25428

D0723532

LAY UP
YOUR TREASURES
IN HEAVEN

Library
Oakland S.U.M.

25428

LAY UP
YOUR TREASURES
IN HEAVEN

Eleanor Tyler Mead

Logos International
Plainfield, New Jersey

Excerpt from the song, "Help Me" by Larry Gatlin. Copyright © 1972 by Combine Music, Inc. Used with permission. All rights reserved.

Excerpt from the song, "Heaven Sounds Sweeter" by Levoy and Cleon Dewey. Copyright © 1973 by Dewey Music Company. Used with permission. All rights reserved.

"To All Parents" a poem by Edgar Guest. Reprinted for Books for Libraries Press, 1970. Distributed by Arno Press, Inc. Used in entirety with permission. All rights reserved.

Excerpt from the songs, "I Didn't Think It Could Be" by Andrae Crouch and "We've Come This Far by Faith" by Albert Goodson. Copyrights with Manna Music, Inc. Used with permission. All rights reserved.

Unless otherwise indicated,
all Scripture quotations are taken
from the King James Version.

LAY UP YOUR TREASURES IN HEAVEN
Copyright © 1977 by Logos International
All Rights Reserved
Printed in the United States of America
Library of Congress Catalog Card Number: 77-89182
International Standard Book Number: 0-88270-257-2
Logos International, Plainfield, New Jersey 07061

To the many people who prayed for us constantly, because through their intercession God gave us the peace that passes all understanding when our three beloved children graduated to glory.

Safely Home

I am home in heaven, dear ones;
All's so happy, all so bright!
There's perfect joy and beauty
In this everlasting light.

All the pain and grief are over,
Every restless tossing passed;
I am now at peace forever,
Safely home in heaven at last.

Did you wonder I so calmly
Trod the Valley of the shade?
Oh! but Jesus' love illumined
Every dark and fearful glade.

And He came Himself to meet me
On that way so hard to tread;
And with Jesus' arm to lean on,
Could I have one doubt or dread?

Then you must not grieve so sorely,
For I love you dearly still;
Try to look beyond earth's shadows,
Pray to trust our Father's will.

There is work still waiting for you,
So you must not idle stand;
Do your work while life remaineth—
You shall rest in Jesus' land.

When that work is all completed,
He will gently call you home,
Oh, the rapture of that meeting,
Oh, the joy to see you come.

(Anonymous)

Preface

All of us, at one time or another, receive life's blows that knock us to our knees. From that vantage point we have two choices. We can either fall on our faces in despair or use the time on our knees to gain God's strength and then get up and go on, stronger than before.

Deep emotional wounds, like physical wounds, can only be healed by a process of deep inner healing. For the born-again Christian this process takes the form of victories, intermingled with setbacks; and even the setbacks when properly put into perspective add up to spiritual growth.

In the case of the death of loved ones we find ourselves asking, "Who is responsible for their death—God, Satan, or just a quirk of fate?" This is just one of the questions that must be resolved with much labored prayer when such a tragedy strikes. When that question is answered and fit into the framework of our understanding, another level in the healing process has been achieved, and a new, unanswered question takes its place.

After three of our children were killed in a car wreck in February of 1976, I felt that God wanted the story told—to be told like it really is. The polarization of thoughts and emotions is real. This is very much a part of a person, even if that person is a born-again Christian, living for the Lord at the time the tragedy strikes, and even though that person continues to maintain his or her close relationship with the Lord. At the same time that there are strong mental battles going on, there is a peace that passes all understanding. Along with the body-wrenching emotional pain, there is the joy of knowing that our loved ones are in the presence of the Lord. In the midst of profound lonesomeness, there is the comforting hope of eternal togetherness through Jesus.

When we add a new word to our vocabulary, we begin seeing that word in print for the first time. Now it isn't that the word hasn't been there all along, it's just that we suddenly begin seeing it because now we comprehend it. The same is true about what God's Word has to say about death. When death hits close to home, we begin to comprehend God's Word as it relates to death and, even though we have read the words before, they suddenly become more meaningful.

This book is meant to give some insight and comfort to those who are in similar situations. Tragedy comes in more forms than death. But always, there is a God-given strength available to us.

This book shows the steps my husband and I took in that first year following our children's deaths. Although arranged according to the sequence of events, the book attempts to reveal the intimate side of the problems encountered in grief, and how we were able to work them out with the Lord. It tells of the mental storms that raged within us and how the Lord brought the calm after the storm.

LAY UP
YOUR TREASURES
IN HEAVEN

Chapter 1

The rain fell harshly as I got ready to leave for court, shortly after telling our daughters good-bye and to have a good day. I noticed that Kim, our sixteen-year-old, who drove the others to school, still had her hair in rollers. It was past their usual time to leave. Melisa, the twelve-year-old, sat patiently waiting. Dave, the thirteen-year-old, was still in his room and Jeff, age fourteen, was sick in bed. My husband's aunt was to take care of Jeff that day, so I thought I had everything in order as I darted to the car in the downpour.

My mind was preoccupied with jury selection and it raced through my opening statement as I made my way downtown in the traffic. That morning, February 17, 1976, at 9:00, I was to begin an important jury trial. My clients, Lloyd and Joyce, were my friends. Lloyd had been my Sunday school teacher when I first committed my life to the Lord. They had been involved in an automobile accident about two years earlier and had been hurt, with Joyce having permanent damage. I wanted to do an especially good job for them.

At the courthouse, I checked to see if my clients were there and if my court reporter had arrived. Then I nervously paced, waiting for the earlier cases to finish and for my husband, David, to arrive. Although we seldom handle cases together, on this one I did need help with jury selection. It sometimes becomes too difficult to try to keep up with each individual's name, occupation, special interests and other information when an attorney is working alone in jury selection.

As nine o'clock approached and David hadn't yet arrived, I became increasingly uptight. To keep from obviously pacing the hall, I strolled into the rest room. I had barely walked through the door when one of the circuit court secretaries came in and said my husband was on the phone. "Oh, no," I thought, "he's calling to tell me that he's late and won't be here to help me."

As I answered the phone I heard my husband say, "Ellie, come home. The children have been in a wreck!" I was suddenly shocked out of my role as a preoccupied lawyer awaiting trial and thrust into a world that seemed so unreal that the back of my mind kept telling me, "It's only a dream and you'll soon wake up." "Are you okay?" I demanded, and David's hesitant reply of, "I don't know," made me realize that they were not all right. I knew the wreck was bad, and that David didn't know if the children were dead or alive.

The next few minutes were the worst of the entire ordeal. It was horrible not to know. I tried calling the hospital and got nowhere. A police officer offered to make a call for me and I watched his expression on the phone. When he got off, he only said, "Are you with anyone?" Although that confirmed my suspicions that at least one of the three children was dead, I still had hopes that not all were dead. I was frantic. I rushed for a phone, trying to get any information. As I picked up the receiver, David called in on another line; he was at the hospital. They had brought in Melisa and she was dead. There it was, I could hear it, and grasp it. My baby, the child I loved with every drop of life in my own body, was dead. I murmured that I'd be right there and mechanically turned to walk out. The judge whose court I was scheduled for was standing at the door and I explained very calmly that my youngest child was dead and I didn't know about the others. It was as though enough of me had died right then and there, that for a while I was merely reacting to stimuli as they were put before me.

When I arrived at the hospital David and his mother

embraced me and told me that all three were dead. They had had a head-on collision with a truck. Although another sharp pain raced through my body, it was as though I was already hurt to the ultimate and the hurt didn't seem to have anywhere else to go.

Once the knowledge that all three were dead had finally taken root within us, God's grace began to take over. Although David and I cried softly together when he first told me all three were killed, from then on, God seemed to have His hand on our hearts. Friends, acquaintances and a dozen ministers came to the hospital. In some cases we found ourselves consoling them. We called the appropriate people, gave interviews to the newsmen that came to the hospital, and generally felt very strong.

Our minister, Billy Roy Moore, of the Lord's Chapel, and a friend, went with us to make funeral arrangements. As we sat at the funeral home, our oldest daughter, Lauri, who was a sophomore at a college across town, very methodically reeled off next of kin, addresses, and other information to the funeral director. It was obvious that she too was experiencing God's strength and grace, combined with the God-given anesthetic that seems to appear at a time like this. I loved her so much as I watched her take command.

We all decided that we were simply planting the shells of what had been our children, and very quickly agreed to have simple caskets with the lids closed. It would not really be our children in those caskets; rather Kim, Dave and Melisa, as we knew them, were with the Lord.

Chapter 2

"God's will, nothing more, nothing less, nothing else." The principal of Pioneer Christian Academy where our children attended school had found those words written in Kim's Bible. Melisa had it written in her Bible too. Those words seem to be the guiding force that led us on. The classmates at school stood on those words; the family members had them indelibly imprinted on their minds.

The morning after the wreck, the school had a memorial service for our children which was covered by both the newspaper and television. What an opportunity to be a witness, yet another part of me cried out, "Jesus, when I said use me, I didn't mean like this."

There were songs by the classmates, words by the principal, and a short sermonette by a minister whose wife was the assistant principal. I knew this had to stir up old wounds for them also in that their daughter had died a year earlier. For this reason, I deeply appreciated their participation in the service. Next, David came to the platform to say a few words. "Gang," he said, "we know many of you by your faces and others we have only heard about around the supper table."

My mind floated back to many happy times we had around the table. During the week there would be the six of us, the four kids at home and David and I. Then on weekends Lauri always came home from college. How many times David and I praised the Lord because we had such good kids. The worst problems we had as parents were an occasional quarrel and periodic messy rooms. We never had to face the problems many families do with a houseful of teenagers. All our children were born-again Christians who didn't take dope, run with a bad crowd or give us any discipline problems. As a family we were close and had fun together. Usually when kids get to be teenagers, mom and dad become like the plague, but our kids wanted to be with us. David and I used to tease them by saying that in order to be alone, we had to sneak out. Lauri and Kim were the only ones who dated, and it was not unusual for them to want us to double date with them.

Each night at supper we heard what went on in school that day. Melisa and Dave were always bubbling, each trying to talk first. They were very much into the junior high scene and both were good students, leaders in their class and, in general, kids with personality. If there was a class election, club election, representative election, ball team to be chosen or a play to be put on, we knew that at least part, if not all of our kids, would be picked, not because they were so special but because their personalities flowed. Yet each was a very definite individual.

My mind was pulled back to the memorial service as I heard David say, "Our kids were ready to live, but they were also ready to die; they had made Jesus Christ their personal Savior." Yes, I thought, they were ready to live and my thoughts strayed back to three days earlier. Melisa had been chosen for the queen's court of the junior high banquet. Dave was a big basketball player. Since Melisa had no special boy friend and Dave had no special girl friend they decided to go with each other's best friend. This was their first boy-girl outing. Melisa had a long formal, her first, and her long, dark hair was accented by her beautiful, big, black eyes and she looked gorgeous. Dave had a new leisure suit and was proud of his new status in puberty. Their evening was a rousing success and they had a ball.

On the afternoon of the big banquet, Dave and his buddy, John, who was also Melisa's escort, had a basketball game. The whole family attended to cheer them on to victory and excitement was in the air the entire day. John came home with Dave to get ready for the banquet, and when we arrived, off the two boys went—of all things—to play basketball outside.

No basketball for Melisa though; she was having her first "dress-up" experience in junior high. She was off to get beautiful. She set about putting clear polish on her nails, getting her hair washed and set, having her dress laid out and taking care of other details.

When the boys finally decided it was time to take a shower and get ready, it was so much fun to go from room to room.

Lauri was home from college and she was fixing Melisa's hair "just right" and Melisa was beaming from ear to ear. "Can I wear just a little eye shadow, mom?" she asked on one of my trips to her room.

"Well-l-l," I answered.

Lauri interjected, "Now, mom, this is something special."

"Okay," I replied. Melisa's happy giggle assured me that I had given the correct answer.

The boys were being "cool." They didn't want to seem excited, and wanted to act like this party was an everyday occurrence, but they sure did stand in front of the mirror. When they finally emerged from their room, they smelled like a walking Old Spice ad. My last warning to the boys was, "Now act like gentlemen." And it didn't go unheeded. Dave yelled through the door, "Hey, Melisa, don't forget to wait for us to open the door, so we can be gentlemen." Then came a giggle from all.

The finishing touches were added and Melisa came out of her room, ready for the excitement of the evening that lay ahead. "You look beautiful, Melisa," I said with a smile, my heart bursting with pride.

"Thank you," she smiled back, in an unfamiliar ladylike pose. I'll never forget the smiles that we gave to one another.

21

I drove the three to pick up Cathy who was Dave's date and Melisa's best friend. We took pictures of the two couples and then we were off to the banquet. It seemed so strange to see the boys jump ahead to open doors.

They giggled for most of the ride to school. The girls reminded the boys to give them their arms, and the boys teasingly told the girls that they guessed they would just play basketball until this party was over and then meet them afterward.

Melisa was so proud to be in the queen's court as was Cathy, Dave's date. They had a crowning, pictures, and other coronation festivities. After the party they all came back to our house to snack, and giggle some more. As usual, the girls put on jeans and they all played basketball.

Yes, they were so full of life and they were not willing to let one second of it pass them by. But David was right, they were ready to die too. They had accepted the Lord and had committed their lives to Him. They were young when they had committed their lives to God; Melisa was eight, Dave was nine and Kim was thirteen. Dave and Melisa accepted the Lord at a church service and Kim accepted Him at camp. During those few years as Christians they had made a lot of blunders, as we all do, yet Christ was the center of all to them. The girls were more open to worship the Lord, yet in the quiet talks that Dave and David would have at bedtime, Dave so often expressed his faith in God. For years, when she was little, Melisa expressed her love for Christ in her pictures that she brought home from art class. As she got older this graduated to more sophisticated decoupage.

Loving God didn't hinder Dave from all the sports activities, school spirit and plain fun, nor did it hinder Melisa from boy-girl talk, school enthusiasm, or being in love with Donny Osmond. Yet, on the other hand, none of these activities and interests, which are a normal part of growing up, hindered them from loving their God. He was a part of their life, not just on Sunday but on a daily basis.

Sometimes adults will think that children are too small to comprehend a Christian experience. They will assume children just go to heaven because they are children. Adults tend to think that a saving experience is merely a Sunday school experience. But children can and do accept Christ as their personal Savior and center their lives around Christ. I know our children did. Sometimes children accept Him far more openly and freely than adults, which is probably why God tells us to come unto Him as the little children, without hang-ups and hindrances.

Jesus was an active force in the lives of even Melisa and Dave, the youngest two. On the Sunday before she went to heaven Melisa said to my sister, "Aunt Debby, how much is 10 percent of two dollars?" When Deb replied, "Twenty cents," Melisa said, "Golly, that's not very much."

Deb asked, "Melisa, are you thinking of tithing?"

Melisa replied, "Yes, but God deserves more than twenty cents a week."

Deb explained to her that what belonged to God was 10 percent and anything over that was a love offering to God. Melisa finally decided she needed to tithe regularly but that it was her responsibility to see that God got more than twenty cents a week. Even a twelve-year-old can understand the relationship between him and God, and the concept of responsibility to our Creator. This isn't a Sunday-morning-only awareness, but a core-of-life kind of awareness.

Dave would say, when we would talk of the Second Coming, "Yes, but I hope He doesn't come right away because I've been praying for so-and-so who hasn't gotten saved yet and I don't want Him to come until that person gets saved." Even at thirteen there can be a concern for the salvation of others, supported by prayers from that young person. God hears those prayers as easily as He hears the

23

most profound prayers of the most articulate saint.

A few years ago, David's parents retired and moved to Nashville. When they came, Dave asked, "Grandma, will you have a Bible club?"

She had had one in Pennsylvania for years, and now offered, "Dave, I will if you get anyone to come." Dave, Melisa and Jeff took off to the neighborhood and soon rounded up enough kids to have a Bible club, which grew so quickly that in the next year it had to be divided into two meetings. It still is going on now with two teachers.

When it came Dave's time to choose a song, he would choose either "Wounded for Me" or "Lord, I Believe." One day, Dave's grandmother said, "Dave, how come those are the only songs you ever choose?"

He said, "Grandma, they tell the story of Jesus just like I believe."

If ever there was a fantastic Christian it was Kim. When other teenagers put her down for her faith, she smiled and praised the Lord. When she sang, "Oh, I want to see Him, look upon His face," she meant it with every fiber of her being. Her very existence each day gave forth the essence, "Jesus lives within me." Yet she was far from being obnoxious about her Christianity. She carried no condemning spirit or "holier than thou" attitude. We knew that when Kim died and approached the throne she had achieved her life's ambition.

By the time she was fifteen, we found that we only communicated with Kim on an adult level. She had a perception of life, people, and God, that had reached a point of maturity that few adults achieve. She knew who she was and where she was going. She too was ready to live, but was she ever prepared to die!

Chapter 3

By the second day, the house was full of people. Food, plants and the mail began pouring in. We received so many beautiful letters, cards and gifts from people we knew and many from people whom we didn't know. It was the prayers of hundreds of people that sustained us. We became aware that heaven was very close. Later we were to read Helen Steiner Rice's words concerning death, "Heaven seems a little nearer, God's promise a little clearer, and His love a little dearer."

During this time heaven seemed so close that we felt we could reach up and grab a handful. It made us aware of how much we wanted to be there too.

The power of prayer from a multitude of people we knew and many we didn't know did sustain us those first few days. We were able to sleep those first few nights and held up quite well at the funeral home. We found that in many cases we were consoling other people.

By this time radio, television and newspapers had picked up on the children's deaths and it became a human interest item in most of Middle Tennessee. A local television station had covered the memorial service at school and most of Nashville had heard David's words, "Our kids were ready to live, but they were also ready to die." The newspaper first carried stories of the wreck, then the memorial service, then the funeral itself.

As it always happens when a situation becomes news, we got a few crackpot phone calls and letters. They ranged from statements that the kids were killed because we go to church on Sunday instead of Saturday, to statements that God killed them to punish us for our sins. Well, one thing they were right about is that we do fail God and sin. What so many people fail to realize is that when we accept Jesus, His sacrifice for our sins becomes forgiveness for our sins—past, present and future.

When we accept Jesus there is a dual nature within us. Sure, the part of us that is of the Lord cannot sin, but the old man is still very much a part of us and does cause rebellion against the ways of the Lord. Paul spoke of the dilemma within him, "I really want to do what is right, but I can't. I do what I don't want to—what I hate. I know perfectly well that what I am doing is wrong, and my bad conscience proves that I agree with these laws I am breaking. But I can't help myself, because I'm no longer doing it. It is sin inside me that is stronger than I am that makes me do these evil things" (Rom. 7:15-17 TLB). Then Paul went on to say, "Who will free me from my slavery to this deadly lower nature? Thank God! It has been done by Jesus Christ our Lord. He has set me free" (Rom. 7:24-25 TLB).

Jesus not only forgives but forgets. Or as the Bible says, "For I will be merciful to their unrighteousness, and their sins and their iniquities will I remember no more" (Heb. 8:12).

Even David and I marveled at the amount of strength that we had those first few days and when it came time to plan the funeral we knew it had to be a praise gathering. We asked ourselves, "If the children could plan their own funeral, what would they do?" We knew they would all say, "Don't make it sad because we are with Jesus now, so praise the Lord." We also knew that they would tell us, "We want an altar call given." We knew that Kim in her very dignified, ladylike way would say, "Oh, praise the Lord," while Melisa in her very undignified manner would shout out, "All right, that's a blast," if anyone accepted the Lord as personal Savior at their funeral. Little were we to realize how great an impact the funeral would have.

26

For the pallbearers we asked many of our minister friends from various churches and denominations. One thing we had learned as Christians is that there is no longer a denominational barrier between born-again Christians. We are all part of the body of Christ. We also chose some of the kids' friends from school and some of our friends. Selecting eighteen pallbearers was not the difficult task that one might assume it would be.

Next we had to choose a speaker. The kids went to a different church than the one David and I attended, although we visited each other's churches periodically. We loved the church where the children attended in that we had committed our lives to the Lord there. However, we had felt the Lord wanted us at the Lord's Chapel. The children attended Evangel Temple, where Brother Jimmy R. Snow was the pastor. They were involved with the church's teaching programs, Grand Old Gospel, and other activities.

We finally decided to have three ministers speak. We selected our minister, Rev. Billy Roy Moore of the Lord's Chapel, Rev. Jimmy R. Snow of Evangel Temple, and a good friend of ours, Rev. Pat Dupree, of The Way Ministries, a youth ministry.

Among our dearest and closest friends were Henry and Hazel Slaughter, who are in gospel music and regularly appear with the Bill Gaither Trio in concert. They are fine Christian people and we would have liked for them to have provided the music for the funeral, but they were in California. Although we had many friends in the gospel music field, we selected a non-professional, Cathy, from our church. We decided that the song "Amazing Grace" contained a verse which was appropriate, "When we've been there ten thousand years, Bright shining as the sun, we've no less days to sing God's praise Than when we'd first begun." We knew that someday soon we would all be together again singing God's praise for eternity. The

27

knowledge of that great reunion gave us victory over sorrow.

The day of the funeral was warm for February, fifty and sixty degrees. The sun shone brightly and early signs of spring were beginning to appear. It was then that we realized that spring is God's constant reminder of eternal life. The earth's foliage seemingly dies in the winter only to burst forth in the spring, far more beautiful than when fully bloomed at a later season.

Between six hundred and seven hundred people attended the funeral. Brother Snow spoke of Kim's favorite verses which she shared on her recent trip to Israel. The previous September Kim had wanted to go to the Holy Land. We had told her we would help her get a loan, but that she had to get a job and repay the money. She made the trip, loved every second of it, and then came home and went to work at McDonald's to pay for it.

"I actually walked where Jesus walked," she'd say, out of deep thought. "I stood on the shore of Galilee," she would exclaim, almost still too astonished to believe it was true. One of the trips she enjoyed most was her visit to Petra, the hidden city where the Bible predicts the Israelites will flee during the tribulation (Jer. 49:16). Kim enjoyed being at Petra because she felt God's presence was extremely strong there.

She made her trip up Golgotha where Jesus was crucified and looked down on the same city that Jesus looked down on and loved. From the Mount of Olives she looked at the sealed Eastern Gate that He will return through and she cried for joy.

The passage of Scripture that most impressed Kim as she stood on the Mount of Olives tells about Jesus right after He gave communion to his disciples. In this passage, Jesus and the group go to the Mount of Olives and sing a hymn. Then Jesus tells His disciples that they will be offended because of

Him. But Peter protests that he would never be offended. When Jesus continues and tells Peter that he will deny Him, Peter protests more vehemently and tells the Lord that he would die for Him and never deny Him.

This we know, Peter did deny Jesus that night, the night of Jesus' arrest. Kim knew that there is a little of Peter in all of us. We say, "Lord, I want your will in my life," then we do our own. We can mouth words of intent to live so good for God, then immediately blow it. Thank God, though, Jesus is the same today as yesterday. Just as He forgave Peter, He forgives us. Kim was impressed that the angel told Mary Magdalene, "Tell his disciples *and Peter* that he goeth before you into Galilee" (Mark 16:7, italics mine). Jesus loved Peter enough to ask for him by name even though Peter had failed Him. Isn't it great that the same Jesus lives today?

Before we accepted the Lord, our definition of a Christian was someone who went to church, and didn't smoke, drink or cuss. We had no concept of the inward relationship with Jesus. We only saw the outward, physical actions. We couldn't understand that born-again Christians, like Peter, were fallible. We thought that if a Christian failed, then he was a hypocrite. I'm glad we were so terribly wrong. It is the relationship with the Lord that makes the difference. If being good got us to heaven then the Pharisees would have been there long ago.

Brother Moore spoke of what the Bible says about heaven and born-again Christians. "The Bible tells us of the streets of gold and the mansions," said Brother Moore, "but it's Jesus I want to see. I want to join with multitudes in heaven and sing praises to Jesus," he went on.

Pat Dupree's words were to ring through our ears from that day forward and probably will until we die. "Lay up for yourselves treasures in heaven . . . For where your treasure is, there will your heart be also" (Matt. 6:20-21). How the words have had meaning. Our treasure consists of the things we love most in life. Three of our treasures are in heaven and a part of us, the heart of us, is there also. Those treasures are partially what has induced the intense desire in us for the swift return of our Lord Jesus Christ. Sometimes we want to go home so bad to see our Lord and to see our children.

Pat also put into words other things we knew, but had not yet verbalized. "The ultimate goal of a born-again Christian," began Pat, "is to be in the presence of Jesus. Dave, Melisa and Kim have reached their ultimate goal." Suddenly David and I became acutely aware that as parents we had been a success. We had brought these three children into the world, they had now left it and were dwelling in the house of the Lord forever.

Cathy's beautiful voice singing "Amazing Grace" and "Because He Lives" seemed to fill every inch of the room. How beautiful it was to hear a very soft murmur throughout the various rooms as the people whispered, "Praise the Lord," "Thank You Jesus," and "Hallelujah." We really were having a praise gathering and God was directing it.

Next, Brother Snow gave an altar call. It was a strong altar call and my first thought was, that's too pointed, too directed, too hard. Then I realized we gave this service to God, for Him to do with according to His will and, if He is in charge, then I shouldn't be telling Him how to run it. In response, people throughout the numerous rooms raised their hands, but only those in the main room could get to the front. Seven people came forward from the main room, knelt in front of the three caskets and gave their hearts to the Lord. Then I knew the altar call was just as God had planned. One of those who came forward was a cousin whom Kim had long been praying for. Another was Melisa's best girl friend. I could hear Kim up there saying, "Oh, praise the Lord," and Melisa saying, "All right, that's a blast!"

Afterward, there was a handful of those who were very

critical and accused us of turning the funeral into a revival. Amidst this criticism we both felt if that is what happened, how grateful to God we are that He used our children's deaths in such a wonderful way for the upbuilding of His kingdom. They were and still are something special.

At the funeral home a very dear friend of ours gave us an essay to read. She was an older lady whose son had died several years earlier. Little did we realize that within a short time this dear saint of God would also go to her heavenly home.

When we got home from the funeral I sat down and read the essay my friend had given to me.

What Is Dying?

I am standing upon the seashore. A ship at my side spreads her white sails to the morning breeze and starts for the blue ocean. She is an object of beauty and strength and I stand and watch her until at length she hangs like a speck of white cloud just where the sea and sky come down to mingle with each other. Then someone at my side says, "There! She's gone."

Gone where? Gone from my sight—that is all. She is just as large in mast and hull and spar as she was when she left my side, and just as able to bear her load of living freight to the place of destination. Her diminished size is in me, not in her; and just at that moment when someone at my side says, "There! She's gone," there are other eyes watching her coming, and other voices ready to take up the glad shout, "There she comes!"

And that is dying. (Author unknown.)

Chapter 4

After the funeral we felt we would like to go away for a few days. Jeff was nearly over the flu or whatever it was that kept him home on the day of the wreck. Jeff was the middle child and since he and Dave were only thirteen months apart, they did almost everything together. Therefore, we felt it would take some adjusting on his part. Only later were we to learn how God interceded and how easily his adjustment would come. We should have known by his first words when he was told that his brother and two of his sisters were dead. He replied, "Well, they're with Jesus."

A friend offered us rooms in Daytona Beach, so we invited a friend of Jeff's to go along and headed south. As the miles rolled along, our thoughts now had time to settle on all that had happened. Now we knew what it was like to hurt so bad emotionally that your body hurts. We knew what it was like to ache until you think your insides would spill out, yet at the same time to have a peace.

Songs on the radio seemed to declare our sorrow. "The Way We Were" was popular and being played by all the stations. As I listened to the words, my mind was flooded with memories—memories of the way we were. My mind would go back to the scene of nightly laughter and teasing around the supper table. As the song continued, I knew that some of my memories were beautiful and that some of them were painful. I wondered what painful memories we might choose to forget. I was thankful that we had no regrets about our relationship with the children. We loved them and they knew it. Yet I also wondered what we would forget as the years pass. Would we ever forget the sound of their laughter or the feel of their arms around us?

We stopped at several points of interest on the trip, joked with the boys in the back seat and generally enjoyed our various tours. Yet always present with us was a lonesomeness. We could praise God that they were in His presence, yet we missed them so much. In shops I still found that eyes would search out for something that they would like and I would have to remind myself that as human beings they existed no more.

The first night at Daytona Beach I hurt so badly that I truly felt as though my insides would push out of me. I lay on the bed and took my Living Bible and prayed. I have never been one who could just open the Bible and find the appropriate verse, but this night I prayed and told God how bad I hurt and asked Him to speak to me through His Word. At random, I opened my Bible to 1 Corinthians, chapter 15, and began reading. One thing I immediately recognized is that when you are in a situation, you have the ability to comprehend God's Word relating to that situation as you never could before. This was how it was with me and chapter 15 of 1 Corinthians. I had read it before, yet I began seeing new things because now I could comprehend it.

I read that if we believe that Christ was resurrected from the dead then we must believe that the dead in Christ will also be resurrected; for if there is no resurrection for the dead then Christ must still be dead, and if He is still dead, then all preaching is worthless and hopeless. Paul went on to say that if being a Christian is only of value for us during life then we are the most miserable of creatures and should just go out and have a good time and eat, drink and be merry. Not the case though, says Paul, for Christ will defeat all enemies, the last of which is death, and all who are related to Christ will rise.

Then God let me understand a little about what the children were like. Through Paul's writings I began to comprehend that a kernel of corn, a grain of wheat, a petunia

34

seed, or any other kind of seed, has to die and be planted in the earth. What comes from that dead seed is something far different and more beautiful than the original seed. The tall cornstalk with its might and beauty is far different from that dried-up seed.

Since flesh and blood, with its weaknesses, can't inherit the kingdom of heaven, it is only when that body seemingly dies that it can become the magnificent spiritual body that can inherit God's kingdom.

This passage also raised some questions which remained unanswered until much later. As weeks passed I found that I was asking God, "What are they really like in this new spiritual body? What do they do all day? How do they think?" After some time of asking, God showed me something.

On our front porch we have an old-fashioned farmhouse swing. On many warm evenings our family would gather after dark, on the front porch, in the warm, summer night air. Those who were able to fit on the swing would fill it up first, and the others would bring up lawn chairs. We would sit in the stillness of the night and talk about what the Lord was doing in our lives, or about things in general. There would be much laughter, teasing and good fellowship.

One day after returning from Florida, I sat alone in that swing, silently swinging and thinking. Our dog, Scrounge, came up and put his head in my lap for some petting. Scrounge has been in the family for five years. Scrounge loved the children and they loved him, and I am sure that he is aware that they loved him, and I am sure that he is aware that the kids don't come home from school to play with him any more. Yet, if I spent the whole day trying to explain to Scrounge why the children were no longer there, and what happened, he wouldn't know any more when I finished than when I began. He only understands dog things, not human things. God finally showed me it was the same with me. If He spent all day explaining to me about the children's lives now,

I still wouldn't know because my mind is only capable of comprehending on a human level and not on a spiritual level. With the utmost simplicity, God helped me to understand.

This new understanding began to develop that night in the Florida hotel room. Other wonderful insights were imparted to me that evening also. While reading 1 Thessalonians 4:13, the Lord seemed to say, "Ellie, I want to tell you about your dead children so you and David won't be like those who have no hope."

I knew what God meant. We had seen funerals where the relatives and friends were not born-again Christians and for many of these people there was a feeling of hopelessness. We could sense that to these few there was not a sense of victory, or a hope of transformation to spiritual beings in death, but rather a feeling of finality, a feeling that death was the end. "Thank God," I thought, "that we no longer have that sense of despair that we would have had prior to making Jesus the focal point of our life." How sad it is to see those who have no hope develop into bitter beings trying so desperately to relieve their own pain when they lose a loved one. Bitterness seems like a cancer that destroys the innermost parts of those who, without the blessed peace that Christ gives, want to blame man or God, and curse man or God, and hurt others for their own sorrow's sake.

I finished reading what the Word of God said about my children rising to meet the Lord first and how we would be "caught up" to meet the Lord. I lay there for a while thinking of what I had read and I wondered about Christ being the first-fruits. I wondered what the children's numbers would be when they rose. I remembered that some preacher we had once heard said Jesus was referred to as "the only begotten Son" before His death and resurrection, but never afterward. After the resurrection He was referred to by other terms, such as first-born, first-fruits, and the second Adam.

Before I fell asleep, I thanked God for giving me a

comprehension of His Word that I had never known before. I realized that no man could have given such explicit answers to my questions as God gave to me through His Word. Then I began to understand the meaning of the biblical admonition, "Comfort one another with these words" (1 Thess. 4:18). There is no way to know the pain nor the peace that comes to a born-again child of God, who loses a loved one, unless you have experienced it.

The following days, as we walked along the beach, our eyes seemed to play tricks on us and we would momentarily think we saw one of the children. I found myself searching the waves, looking for Melisa to appear with her long, dark hair cascading over her slender body that was beginning to take the form of the young woman that she was fast becoming.

Occasionally it would seem as though the chubby blond boy jumping the waves was our Dave. We had seen him so many times before being knocked down by the waves, his knees being scraped upon the ocean floor, then turning around more determined than ever to go back again and conquer the next wave.

Since northern Florida is only about an eight-hour drive from Nashville, we had made the trip often, and had a whole network of memories of our ocean visits stored up in our brain.

In the evenings, David and I walked along the beach alone in the moonlight. One evening, David shared with me a dream he had about one month earlier. In this dream, he was standing alone and sobbing at the edge of the ocean. Since he and I have shared nearly everything since our marriage began, he awoke with a fear that something might happen to me.

That night as we stood barefoot in the sun-warmed sand and the waves lapped at our ankles, we held each other tightly and cried. We missed and longed for the children so badly, yet how good it was to truly love each other.

Chapter 5

It was going on two weeks since the children were killed; the illusory world of Florida had to be put aside. It was time to put our law practice together and time to attempt to redefine our family roles.

We had a lot of things going for us including love, which made things far easier than they would have been if that element had been missing. Yet we all knew that there would have to be many readjustments. Lauri was still in college except on weekends, which meant that in place of the hustle and bustle of a houseful of teenagers, there would be only three people in a very quiet house.

Most of all, we dreaded our first meal at home and consequently put it off for a while by eating out. As all things must eventually be faced, Jeff went back to school and found it was much easier than he expected. David and I discovered we both had court the first day back, so we went together. The majority of the attorneys, clerks, and other employees avoided our eyes as nearly as possible except for a few brave souls who had the courage to come up and offer their condolences. I guess perhaps the majority of people we encountered those first weeks were afraid to confront us. In some cases it was almost as though they were thinking, "If I don't mention it, maybe they'll forget it."

Since I am one who prefers to get difficult tasks out of the way, I went right to the job of cleaning out the children's rooms and getting rid of their clothes. As I worked I discovered many assurances that the Lord had moved in the children's lives right before their deaths to leave us important messages when they were gone.

In Dave's room I began working and found myself

confronted with football trophies, baseball trophies, the ball with which he hit his home run and various other valuables of his. In the midst of all this I found his Children's Living Bible. At random I opened it and began reading what he had underlined. To my astonishment, I read, "Don't store up treasures here on earth where they can erode away or may be stolen. Store them in heaven where they will never lose their value, and are safe from thieves. If your profits are in heaven your heart wil be there too" (Matt. 6:19-20 TCLB).

"Yes, Dave," I thought, "you, one of our treasures, are indeed in heaven where you definitely won't lose your value and Satan can never try to steal your salvation from you now. And, Dave," my thoughts continued, "our hearts are there with you also."

In Melisa's room, under the bed, was her warehouse for junk, and cleaning that was an enormous task. In fact, the area under her bed was a family joke. Each year at Halloween we had a family ritual. When the kids had returned from their trick-or-treat outing and had sufficiently surveyed their loot, we would light the jack-o'-lanterns, turn out the lights and begin a ghost story. The way this worked was that we would sit on the floor in a circle and one of us would start some preposterous tale. When that person's imagination would run out, he would raise that inflection of his voice and say, "And then. . . ."

This was the clue for the next person in the circle to pick up and go on with his made-up story. Each year the boys would get around in their story to a point where the ghost was chasing them and would be just about to catch them but would accidentally fly under Melisa's bed and become entrapped in the junk. The story would usually end when their tale would get so outlandishly ridiculous that they would roll over on their side, on the floor, doubled up in laughter.

As I stood up from digging under her bed, I looked in

Melisa's mirror. There, stuck under the frame, was a tiny Bible opened to this verse, "I am the resurrection, and the life: he that believeth in me, though he were dead, yet shall he live: And whosoever liveth and believeth in me shall never die" (John 11:25-26).

On the opposite page I read, "For God so loved the world, that he gave his only begotten Son, that whosoever believeth in him should not perish, but have everlasting life" (John 3:16). These verses seemed to be God's way of saying to me, "I just want to confirm to you that they are with Me and now have eternal life."

Kim literally had mounds of Bible study material, books, teaching tapes, and Bibles in her room. Her Bible was so marked up that it was almost as though the verses that weren't underlined were the ones that stood out. If there is any validity in the saying, "If your Bible is in good shape, you're not," then Kim was indeed in good shape. On nearly every page she had written on the margins, and the front and back covers were loaded. She had written down "the Romans road to salvation," steps of faith, Scriptures on fasting, and much, much more.

Amongst the many underlined verses in Kim's Bible, I particularly noticed these, "For I am persuaded, that neither death, nor life, nor angels, nor principalities, nor powers, nor things present, nor things to come, Nor height, nor depth, or any other creature, shall be able to separate us from the love of God, which is in Christ Jesus our Lord" (Rom. 8:38-39).

One thing I became acutely aware of, as I was reading through Kim's Bible, is that the stories of the Bible were not inserted merely for telling us about a happening that occurred at a former time but rather they were put there to have meaning for us today. For instance, the Book of Job is not in the Bible simply to tell us of Job's afflictions, but rather it is there to be a guiding force for us today. Paul's letters to the various churches were meant not merely as a guide to the local churches of his time, but also as a basis for us to grow into a mature relationship with the Lord today.

The feelings of anger, fear, joy, love, hate, resentfulness, sorrow, happiness, loneliness, togetherness, despair, frustration, excitement, greed, lust, and forgiveness have already been experienced by someone before us. God uses His Word to minister to us when we are in a similar situation. God wants us to know that others before us made it through with peace, the kind of peace that only God can give.

Those messages that I found in the children's rooms gave me an additive of peace. If anyone would have asked prior to the wreck, "What would you do if three of your children were killed?" I probably would have answered, "I couldn't take it." But here we were not only taking it, but being able to praise the Lord in it.

Spring came early this particular year. By the end of February a few courageous daffodils appeared around the neighboring yards and along country roads.

This was the time of year that we had all loved most. Spring in the South is magnificent. The colors of the magnolias, azaleas, and forsythia create a wonderland of beauty throughout the countryside and on suburban streets.

Our home sits on a high hillside which our northern friends call "Mead's Mountain." We can look across the valley to the next row of high hills and see all of nature's beauty.

Those first few weeks were so strange and almost unrealistic, as though we would soon wake up. The physical appearance of the world was beautiful. Yet somehow, at first, the prettier the scene was, the more intense the hurt was. It was an odd feeling that when he became emotionally involved in something beautiful, the ache of our loss and our lonesomeness came more to the surface. The more we had loved a past experience of beauty, the more we hurt at similar aesthetic sights. To watch the sun go down behind

42

the neighboring hills, with its rosy hue on the new spring buds, became almost too difficult to bear.

The smell of freshly cut grass and the sound of birds singing in the morning would remind me of earlier springs.

There was our first spring in Tennessee. In the spring of 1970 we had decided to make suburban Nashville our home. From the first day we moved to Tennessee we all loved it. The country was so very beautiful, and the people were our kind of people. Because of the difference in climate, we would sometimes wish for a day of northern snow—but no more than a day. In the South, the children thought it was great fun in the winter because the schools closed when the first snowflake would fall. We moved to Madison and found a genuine warmth in our new found friends and neighbors, a warmth that we had never known before.

David and I were still in law school, both of us trying to work days and go to school nights. With children, it wasn't easy. Without the help of the kids, we couldn't have made it. When we finally earned our doctorate of jurisprudence, the kids had earned it too.

Law school was a second career for both of us. David had been a high school principal in Michigan. Although we were not committed Christians and didn't live for the Lord then, we still knew He had a place in our lives. When we first considered going to law school after our youngest child had started school, we asked God to open the doors if law school was where we should be. We passed our law school admission tests, got accepted at the first place we applied, which was in Detroit, and so off to school again we went.

After entering law school we discovered that one should go to school in the state where he intends to practice. Since we had always wanted to live in the South, we decided it was time to make the break, so we sold our house and transferred to a law school in Nashville. We really feel now that God was directing us to Nashville all along, because it is here that we found Him.

Then there was the spring of 1971. That was the spring we had committed our lives to the Lord. When we moved to Tennessee we both had a desire to get into a good church. We had no concept at this time of getting into God. As the year progressed we began to half-heartedly look for a church. We visited around and found nothing except formality. Formality was all that either of us had ever known in a church, but we knew there must be something more than this. We had no idea what it was that we were looking for. In the spring we decided to go to Evangel Temple, a church near our home, and give it a try. I had seen an article in a neighborhood shopper's guide about Evangel Temple, and the same week someone from the church had invited David to attend. Within minutes after we entered that Sunday morning, all of our mouths were open and we all stared at each other in disbelief at what was taking place. In other churches we had recited form prayers, heard Scripture read, and recited creeds, but these people were actually, unashamedly, openly loving and worshiping the Lord. We had never experienced this before. The Spirit of the Lord was there and we could actually feel Him. It is almost a frightening experience to know the Spirit of the Lord is really with you, when you become aware of it for the very first time in your life.

In our lifetime, David and I had been to hundreds of church services and the children had been to quite a few. I suppose it would be an exaggeration to say we had listened to one out of ten sermons, yet this morning when Rev. Jimmy Snow started preaching, we hung onto every word. When noon came he was just getting warmed up and we didn't mind a bit. In fact, we didn't want it to be over.

When the altar call came, we faced somewhat of a dilemma. I had responded to an altar call when I was fifteen years old and David had asked the Lord into his life at age

44

four, yet both of us knew we had never lived as Christians. We decided not to respond to the altar call, partly out of pride and partly because we supposed we didn't need to.

That week we all talked constantly about church, and the family could hardly wait for Sunday to come again so we could go to church. Now this was certainly something new for us. All of us, including the children, began taking peeks in our Bible that week.

The next Sunday came, and then the next and soon we found ourselves in church three times a week, wishing it were more often. Suddenly the Scriptures came alive. No longer did we just read meaningless words from the epistles of Paul, but now we were a friend to Paul, who lived and breathed and taught and was still teaching us each day.

When we lived up north we played games with God. We knew the children belonged in church, so every Sunday we would leave them at Sunday school and go off to buy the morning paper.

Now we were faced with a new situation. At Evangel Temple the preacher does not allow you to merely warm a pew in complacency, but rather he requires that when you leave the church, you have either said yes to God, or you have said no. You cannot sit on the fence. We knew we had said yes.

We totally committed our lives to the Lord and loved every minute of it. Christianity is a constant learning process but right then it was all new and there was so much to learn. When you first comprehend the Scriptures it is like a child with a new toy. We were in love with God and His Son and it was like being on our honeymoon. It was so beautiful to be able to say, "I've become that new creature in Christ Jesus, just like the Bible says. I don't know when I did exactly, but I know I've changed, I'm different." Like all lasting love affairs, within time we settled down to a good, mature, responsible relationship with the Lord and began a slower, but steady growth.

That spring, my sister came to live with us. Something that happened with her made it easier for me to understand God's wonderful gift of salvation.

Deb and I were, for all practical purposes, each an only child in that I was fourteen years older than she and we were the only children in our family. I graduated from high school early, so she was little when I went away to college. I loved her as if I were another parent rather than a sibling.

At the time she came to live with us, Deb was only nineteen years old. One evening after everyone else had gone to bed she began talking to me. She sat on the floor in front of the TV, cross-legged, while I watched from the couch as she began opening her heart to me. She felt guilty about so many parts of her life, and she had to tell them to someone. That someone was me.

I sat and listened as she poured out her ugly past and when she was through I got up from the couch, sat beside her on the floor, and cradled her in my arms. I said, "Deb, there is nothing you could tell me that would make me love you any less."

It reminded me of a similar but totally different situation that had happened to me earlier in my life. I had some friends, an older couple that for years said I was like a daughter to them. At one point in my life they were told some stories about me. These stories were partly true but they also contained some untruths. It was a different scene though, because what I took for love, wasn't love at all. They turned away from me, and I knew that if they had really loved me, nothing I could have done, had it all been true and more, would have ever changed that love.

God's love isn't fickle, and the realization that we as humans can love another person, as I loved Deb, no matter what, made me realize just how powerful God's love really is. When we accept Jesus and begin confessing our most vile, despicable sins, He doesn't smack His cheek and say, "My gosh, I can't believe it." Occasionally we would like to limit God and think we are so unique that we have found a new sin beyond His forgiveness, but it isn't so. God is big enough not only to forgive all our sins, but there is nothing that we could tell Him that would make Him love us any less. Perhaps all of us have ugly, dark parts of our life. I sure have mine and I'm grateful that God's grace is sufficient to forgive me.

After we got saved, we thought we would have a difficult job getting Deb to go to church with us. However, one day at lunch, David said, "Deb, how about going to church with us Sunday?"

To our surprise she said, "Okay." Within herself she was wondering, "Why did I say that?" One of the most powerful messages I have ever heard was preached that Sunday and Deb accepted the Lord.

The message was about the unpardonable sin. In Matthew 12:31 it says that any sin can be forgiven except the blasphemy against the Holy Spirit. The message concerned how one can blaspheme the Holy Spirit and never be forgiven. The gist of the sermon was that the Holy Spirit will tug at our heartstrings and convict us of our sins. If we refuse to accept the Lord when the Holy Spirit pulls at our conscience, then we become a little hardened to the Lord. When the Spirit again knocks at our door, and the inner part of us tells us we should live for the Lord, but again we refuse because we have too much exciting living to do or whatever the excuse, then upon the next refusal, our heart becomes more hardened. This process continues until at a point we have rejected God so much that He refuses to give us the choice of accepting Him and the Holy Spirit ceases to pull at our conscience. When God stops making an appeal to us to accept Him, we have reached the point of the unpardonable sin. Of course, as long as one is being convicted, he and she has not committed the unpardonable sin.

Later Deb was to go on to be one of the strongest Christians I have known. Our whole family was turned upside down or, better still, right side up.

After Deb had grown a little in her new found faith she invited her friend, Bobby, from home to Nashville for the weekend and, of course, Deb took him to church. Many hours of prayer had preceded this visit.

Bobby too accepted the Lord, but this wasn't the end. Blooming out of mutual love for the Lord grew a love for each other. They were married and began serving the Lord as one. Deb now has an associate degree in religion and she teaches the Bible. Bobby, who has been involved in everything from the bus ministry to the music ministry is now back in college after a stint in the army. They are a delightful Christian couple.

Now it was the spring of 1976, and how grateful we were for the spring five years earlier when David and I had committed our lives to the Lord, in that each of our children soon followed our example, and became born-again Christians too. I must give much of the credit for this feat to the prayers of our mothers.

With spring came Easter, and it suddenly took on a whole new meaning. For years, Easter meant egg dyeing, new clothes, Easter baskets, and a remote acknowledgment that Christ arose from the dead. With my salvation, Easter became a time to praise the Lord for His taking on my sin so that by becoming a child of God I was a joint heir with Him, and could plan on eternal life.

Now Easter acquired a new dimension. Because of His death and resurrection, I can know that there is a resurrection for my children. I can know that my treasures are indeed stored up in heaven.

Christ, the only perfect man, came to earth and became the perfect sacrifice for our salvation in order to complete God's perfect plan. He was the first-born without spot or blemish, as was required by the law.

When Adam and Eve allowed Satan to have a foothold on earth, God could have literally ousted Satan right then and there, but He didn't. Instead He chose to follow His own laws, by redeeming His children. In the Old Testament, the law prescribed the sacrifice of the first-born, unblemished lamb by the priest for forgiveness of sin. This was an impermanent, imperfect sacrifice. In order to have a one time perfect sacrifice for all mankind, God chose the most perfect of all, His Son, without the blemish of sin.

So Jesus fulfilled the Old Testament prophecies. He was cursed, spit upon, and His beard yanked out, was beat with a whip imbedded with pieces of sharp, broken bone, was hung on a cross, had His side pierced, and He died.

But that grave didn't keep Him. He arose from the dead, walked among His people for forty days and ascended to the right hand of the Father.

He left His legacy. He said, "I go to prepare a place for you. . . . that where I am, there ye may be also" (John 14:2-3). Then He also said, "Because I live ye shall live also" (John 14:19).

God, who loved us enough to provide for us the perfect sacrifice for our sins, possesses the same tremendous power today that raised Jesus from the dead. That same power is available to all born-again believers for their resurrection to the place Jesus is preparing for them.

Because of this resurrecting power of God, we know our children too have had their own resurrection day; and they too will dwell in the house of the Lord forever.

Chapter 6

As the weeks began to turn into months, I one day realized that yesterday I didn't cry. Then I knew the healing process had started. We soon found that healing is a process—sometimes a lengthy process—with victories and setbacks. But as with all deep wounds, surface healing is not enough; there must be a deep healing, from the inside out.

Each day was, at first, a series of emotional knives plunging deep in the center of our emotional awareness. So many memories were provoked by different sights and sounds. Even the smells and tastes of the children's favorite foods brought back memories. At first there was the intense pain of such simple things as seeing glimpses of their favorite TV programs, hearing a song that reminded us of them, smelling their brand of hand lotion.

David particularly had difficulty in such simple things as ball games on TV. Dave was quite a sports enthusiast. Monday night football, the World Series, and the Superbowl were all his bag. Dave and David had their ritual of popping corn and settling down together for the big sporting events. We remembered the Superbowl that was played in January before the wreck. Dave had prepared charts to keep up with the winner and finally decided to put names in a hat for each family member to draw to see who would get the winner. Much to his dismay, Melisa, who could not have cared less, drew the Superbowl winner.

Within time, however, some of these memories began to turn to sweet memories. The first fire in the fireplace in the fall brought back warm memories of our Saturday night hot dog and marshmallow roasts. I sat there fondly remembering the mantel lined with Christmas stockings, yet at the same time I dreaded having to pull out the box of Christmas decorations and set aside their stockings.

Part of the growth process came through these memories. One evening, while driving, I began thinking of Melisa, my baby. I'm sure she wouldn't like being called my baby, because she thought she was quite grown up.

Driving along, my mind floated back to the wonderful hours I had spent with her at her 2:00 A.M. feeding as a tiny baby. By the time she came along I was a little older than I had been with the first children and far more appreciative of the new creation of God. During the day there was a hustle and bustle of the other children, the phone, meals, and other activities, but at 2:00 A.M. it was just her and I alone, together. I would feed her, play with her and love her without any interruptions. I loved those times with her.

Then I remembered when she was about one year old and her brother was three. I had made a fire in the fireplace and when I came into the living room to check on them they had gotten the dog basket, set it in front of the fireplace and were both sitting in it watching the fire with his arm around her shoulders and her head leaned against his shoulder and neck. I guess if I had to categorize the most beautiful sights I have ever seen that had to be one of them.

My next thoughts went to Melisa as she started school and her excitement at the end of each day telling me all about her day. From there my thoughts drifted to recent memories of her growing so beautiful and becoming a young woman. Then suddenly I knew my next thought was about the present. I stopped, paused for just a second, and realized that she is now a glorious creature. I knew that I couldn't comprehend exactly what she was like, but I knew she was glorious. As tears streamed down my face, I just kept repeating in my mind, "and now she's glorious." I knew all of them were God's glorious creatures.

As our healing process took place and heaven seemed so

much nearer, our comprehension of death and dying became more vivid. David and I are both physically active and capable of doing most anything our children could do. David used to be a coach and is very good in athletics, so he was better than all of the kids in physical sports. I used to teach swimming and lifesaving, so I was always better than all the kids in swimming, water-skiing, and other aquatics. Although the boys were beginning to surpass my abilities in baseball, basketball, and some other sports, I could still keep up.

I guess I had some of ol' Toby Tyler, my dad, in me. I remembered when I was ten years old and we went to a company picnic. There was a swimming pool with a high diving board. I eyed that high board, wanting to go off of it, but was afraid. Finally, I said to my dad, "I sure wish I could go off the high board."

"Go ahead," he encouraged, "you can do it."

After some consideration, I said, "Daddy, I will, if you will." Since I was a late-in-life child my dad was now fifty-two years old, but it took no hesitation for him to meet the challenge, climb the ladder and dive in. I followed, only to discover that looking down from the top of a high board, it appears four times higher than looking up from the bottom. I mustered up my courage and, unlike my father, jumped in instead of diving.

It was only later that I realized that that was the first time he had been off a high diving board in twenty-five years. How I admired him for meeting my challenge. I always wanted to have that same gutsy determination to meet challenges, so when my kids said, "Hey, mom, how about a game of ball," I always wanted to be there. David was a coach and teacher to them, so we often had family gatherings which involved swimming, ball, bowling, tennis, and other physical activities.

With the children now dead, and we always being able to

do with relative ease anything the kids could do, we began to realize how easy it is to die. Christians, we realized, don't fear death. What Christians do fear is the process of dying. Yet how quickly and easily death came for our children.

We have read so many accounts recently of people who have "died." Most people, born-again Christians and non-Christians alike, seem to recount the separation of their own body. Many accounts tell of a tunnel with a brilliant light at the end of it, and often there are stories of hearing beautiful singing. In all instances that we have read about, the individuals wanted to get to the light and the singing, but they were unable to do so.

This has made us give serious consideration to God's Word, most particularly the Twenty-third Psalm. It says, "Yea, though I walk through the valley of the shadow of death, I will fear no evil: for thou art with me" (v. 4). That there is a shadow mentioned must mean that there is a light, for it is impossible to have a shadow without a light. That light must be Jesus Christ. He is referred to throughout the Bible as the Light. Jesus said, "I am the light of the world" (John 8:12). In Ephesians we are referred to as children of light. The first several verses of the first chapter of John repeatedly refer to Jesus as the Light. Jesus is that light which casts the shadow in the valley of death; yet if we look farther, we see that a Christian walks *through* that valley. I believe that a born-again Christian is allowed to walk through that valley, right to the Light, Jesus Christ, and meet Him face to face. The Christian joins with the millions of other saints who were there before Him, singing God's praises. Since, of course, no one ever recounts having reached the end of the valley and meeting the Light, it must be irreversible when you do meet the Savior. But, then, who would ever want to come back after meeting our Lord face to face.

Since John 3:3 clearly tells us that, "Except a man be born again" (accepts Christ as his personal Savior and makes Him

Lord of his life), "he cannot see the kingdom of God," we know that not all who die will get to meet our Lord Jesus Christ.

There is a book entitled *Vestibule* by Jess Weiss (New York: Ashley Books, 1972). In this book, there is a story by Burris Jenkins, who is now a minister. In it he tells how he came to believe in God as a result of being declared clinically dead, and then being revived. He relates the indescribable light and how he could never reach it and he tells how his soul screamed out, "God, help me."

We are looking forward to the return of our Lord, so that we too can meet Jesus and have one fantastic reunion. It amazes me that I had spent my whole life in church and Sunday school, yet no one bothered to tell me what the Bible says about the Second Coming of Christ. There was minimal lip service given to the Second Coming, but that was all. It was simply mentioned that there would be a second coming at some distant future time. According to the Bible, Christ will appear in the air and all living believers will rise to meet Him. In the twinkling of an eye we will be changed to spiritual beings and joined by those believers who have died. The time when this will occur is not known for certain, but we do know that the Second Coming is when Christ actually sets foot on earth to bind Satan. This victory over Satan will occur at the war to end all wars, the Battle of Armageddon.

My sister, Deb, has recently written a song about the day when the Lord appears and calls us home. It goes like this:

What a great reunion day,
When we'll all be caught away,
And the dead in Christ shall rise,
And we'll be all changed in
Twinkling of our eyes.
Praise the Lord, our hearts will say,
When the Lamb calls, "Come away."
What a day, What a day, What a glorious day.

If we meet the Lord through death, that's fine, but if we meet Him in the sky, that will be even greater. However we get there we are looking forward to seeing Jesus and the kids

Chapter 7

As in all Christian families when victories are being won, Satan was determined to make sure that setbacks came to our family. Before the children's deaths, David and three other Christian men had begun a Christian business and this business began to fail. We soon found ourselves saddled with several thousand dollars of personal indebtedness without sufficient income to meet the needs. Our church, the Lord's Chapel, had decided to pay the funeral expenses. For this we thank God because without their help we would have experienced a financial disaster.

As the days went on and the income didn't meet the outgo we became more tense. Physically we began to be drained. We were working forty to sixty hours at the office, each of us was teaching in a local college two nights a week, and yet we couldn't meet expenses. We were still in debt from law school and setting up our practice and this added financial blow was most devastating.

Both of us began experiencing a sensation of doom. It was as though our bodies were constantly tense, out of fear of what the next second would bring and yet we didn't know exactly of what we were afraid. What we were experiencing was something like the feeling of fear that one has when he walks down a dark road alone at night and hears strange sounds. The only difference was that we had this feeling most of our waking hours. We were unable to sleep well and many nights David would wake up dreaming about the kids.

I became very lonesome. Lauri was gone for the summer and planning to get married. When David and Jeff would go off and do their "male things" together I was never jealous, but it seemed to intensify my lonesomeness. I wanted a girl to tell me about who likes who, and to putter in the kitchen and do "girl things" with me.

Then Satan launched one of his biggest attacks on me. One night I picked up a new issue of the *National Geographic* to thumb through. I began reading an article about some primitive South American tribe. The article told of their burial customs and showed crosses at the grave sites with rags, spotted with dyes, tied to the crosses. According to the article this was to ward off evil spirits and take the soul of the deceased to the afterlife.

My mind began roaming back to things I had learned in college anthropology. All cultures, I had been taught, believed in some form of a god. Most cultures, no matter how primitive, believed in life after death. No, I was reading of a primitive culture, with a cross as a symbol, believing as earnestly as I did in life after death. An argument started within my brain that was to last for several weeks.

It was as though one part of my brain would say, "Look, every culture no matter how pagan has had a god and believed in the afterlife and this Jesus bit is no different. We only believe in it so we don't hurt so bad when our loved ones die." Then another part of my brain would retort, "But we have documented proof that Jesus actually lived and traveled in the area around Jerusalem and either He was all He said He was, or the biggest con man the world has ever seen."

Again, the one part of my brain would argue, "These people used crosses on their graves and they probably never even heard of Jesus, let alone His dying on the cross, and they certainly don't believe their dead are going to be with Jesus." The other part of my mind would reply, "If all the prophecies of the Bible about His birth and ultimate death turned out to be 100 percent true as history has proved, why would we not believe that the prophecies about His going to the Father to prepare a place for us, and about His Second

Coming would also be true?"

My mind waged this type of constant warfare for days and the part of me that seemed like the real me, would get so frustrated about this battle. Here I was, a mature Christian who knew God's Word. I had experienced the reality of being born again. I had seen myself become a new creature in Christ Jesus. I had been able to look back and see that I had developed from the "milk-drinking" Christian, learning the basics, to the "meat-eating" Christian, possessing a deeper knowledge and understanding of God's Word just like the Bible talks about in Hebrews 5:12-14. I knew the Bible personally. Big, burly, loving Peter was my friend. Brilliant, articulate, sensitive Paul was my teacher. I knew I had all my senses and I had developed no mental illnesses, yet Satan was having a heyday playing with my mind. Only by turning this problem over to God and rebuking Satan was I able to stop this battle.

When it was over I realized more clearly the meaning of the saying that it is not so much the situation that changes us, but our reaction to the situation. I was reminded of a story of the twin sons of an alcoholic. One son became a teetotaler and the other became a drunk. When each was asked why he was as he was, they both replied, "What else can I be with my father being an alcoholic?"

When a major alteration, or what the world calls a tragedy, comes into one's life, it doesn't leave us unchanged. We can grow cold and bitter and mad at God or we can grow in God's grace, and give meaning to the tragedy. It isn't the situation itself but our reactions to the situation that change us.

When the battle cries within my brain had subsided, I came out the winner of the bout. I had reached another level of maturity in both my Christian growth and also in my healing process. Satan has different ways of dealing with different individuals, according to their weak areas.

59

Satan's next attack came by way of a magazine article I had written. I submitted it to *Christian Life* magazine before the kids were killed. It is an article about how Satan is using the advertising media to bombard us daily with Satan-oriented symbols. The article told of how Madison Avenue ad men have used sex-oriented words and symbols to tickle our subconscious mind and stimulate our buying by using taboos. With sex being so blatantly displayed, however, the ad men have had to reach for another taboo and are now using what they call death-oriented mechanisms. But a born-again Christian readily recognizes these as Satan-oriented symbols too. My article went on to say that we must combat this carnal garbage by the constant renewing of our minds, by reading God's Word on a daily basis.

I didn't know the fate of my proposed article until the May after the children's deaths. One day I got a call from a friend who said, "I enjoyed your article in the new *Christian Life*." I quickly came home, got my magazine from the mailbox, turned the pages and, there it was, in the May 1976 issue, "How to Keep from Being Manipulated," by Eleanor Tyler Mead.

After the thrill of having my article published subsided I began to wonder, "Did Satan kill the children because I was attacking him?"

The problem then had to be faced—did God take their life, did Satan take their life or did this all just happen? When one faces this type of dilemma, other people can not help very much. Although we asked for no suggestion as to who was the instigator of their fate, people offered "help" anyway. "We must rebuke the devil, because the Bible says he comes to steal, kill and destroy," some would say. "God couldn't will the death of children," others would say. This was a problem we had to work out with the Lord.

It was easy to see that some groups of people were making

a god out of Satan by giving him credit for every negative occurrence. They spent so much time rebuking Satan that they were in fact exalting him. It wasn't too difficult to reason that if we gave Satan credit for the deaths of our children, we were giving him more power than God.

The Bible refers to Satan and his demonic cohorts as authorities of this world. The world that they have authority over is the world system. The Bible says that Christians are not of this world. Certainly we live on the earth, but we are separated from the world system, even though we must operate within it. In the world system money is god, and "Get the other guy before he gets you" is the motto.

These demonic forces are capable of wielding power through the arena of the mind. The attacks from Satan come in the form of depression, anger, anxiety, fears, and other negative emotions. It's from these attacks that we learn that we must stand on the power of God to prevent Satan from getting a foothold.

But what about those who have accepted Jesus as their personal Savior, the ones that Christ said are not of this world? God delivered us from the authority of darkness and translated us into the kingdom of His beloved Son (Col. 1:13). The words *delivered* and *translated* are past tense words. Born-again believers have already been delivered and translated. Satan likes to attack us through the mind, but he is powerless to harm us physically, unless, as with Job, God gives him permission.

After reaching that conclusion, we now had left the propositions that God willed it or it just happened without God's direction. If we, as Christians, commit our lives to God and believe His hand is on our lives in decision-making, and if we believe in his general guidance in our everyday life, doesn't it seem natural that He should be with us most intimately at the times of our physical birth, our spiritual birth and our death? What three times in any life are most important?

The Bible tells us that not one sparrow falls to the ground without God (Matt. 10:29-31). Could a sparrow's death be in God's control while a human's life was not? God says that man is of more value than the sparrows. (v. 31).

When I was a child, my father had a favorite saying, "Tell people that there are a million stars in the sky and they will believe it, but tell them it's wet paint and they will have to touch it to believe it." The same seems true relative to the power of God. If we tell people that the Russians have a satellite that has the capability of photographically scanning America with such clarity that the shingles on my roof can be counted, this is conceivable to most people. However, if we tell most people that God has the hairs on our head counted, often they will scoff. Yet surely if the Russians can count the shingles on our roof from Moscow, God could count the hairs on our head from heaven.

Now does it really make one iota of sense that God would think enough of us to have the hairs on our head counted, then leave something so important as our death and our transformation from a human being on earth to a spiritual being in heaven, up to mere chance or fate?

We know that all things work together for the good of those Who love God, the called ones, according to His purpose (Rom. 8:28). The word *all* cannot be ignored or eliminated from that verse.

We know God to be in control of all things. Just as surely as He is in control of the earth's destiny, so is He in control of man's destiny. God gives us the choice to accept or refuse Him. He doesn't want us to be puppets, but when we commit our lives to Him, we also commit our death and eternal life to Him.

So many circumstances could have been changed and the children would be alive. That road was a winding, country road which was lightly traveled. Why should a truck be on that road at all, let alone just at the right spot on the curve? The wreck occurred at a spot where there were no trees and in a front yard of a country home. Kim could have gone into a skid on the wet pavement, ended up in the yard and learned a good lesson—except for the truck. Kim was always prompt; why was she running late this day? Why did Jeff stay home sick? He rarely gets sick. All these things indicate it was God's plan. Why? I don't know, but perhaps He can use the children more in death than in life.

As time passed the financial problems and burdens didn't lessen much, until we got to the point of thinking that we should perhaps quit law practice. But, of course, the obvious question is, and then what? We were both trained as lawyers and we both did well at our professional skills.

David would at times become very depressed and fought hard against getting mad at God. It was easy, at times, to think that God had turned His back on us. However, all those low times were interspersed with the awareness of God's care. There were times that we led a polarized Christian life. For short periods we would fluctuate back and forth, like pulling petals from a daisy, "He loves me, He loves me not."

At this writing we know there are still valleys to cross, or as David jokingly says, hurdles to hurd, yet past experiences let us know that we will come out on top. We are joint heirs with Jesus. We know the last chapter of the book.

Chapter 8

The Sunday after the kids' deaths we went to our church at the Lord's Chapel. We stood there, a mixture of sadness and gladness, with tears running down our faces as the congregation happily clapped and sang, "I'll fly away, oh glory, I'll fly away. When I die, hallelujah by-and-by, I'll fly away." Then came the song, "When We All Get to Heaven." This was our first lesson in how much work it can be to be in God's house. Realizing that our son and daughters are with Jesus is a painful experience mingled with joy.

When the services were over, Virginia Trimble, whose daughter, Marcia, had been murdered the year before, came to me. She embraced me and said, "Don't you feel special?" I really couldn't comprehend this, but then I knew she had a year's head start on me in her healing process. They too had been a born-again Christian family, all living for the Lord, when Marcia was kidnapped and, later, on Easter Sunday, she was found strangled.

This was my first taste of being comforted by someone who had experienced a similar situation, as is set out in 2 Corinthians 1:4. The words, "Don't you feel special," rolled around and around in my head, but within time I began to understand what she meant.

We knew that many people got saved at the funeral and soon we began to learn of others. Jeff's best buddy at school accepted the Lord, and his parents also began going to church with him. Stories began drifting in from other people who came to the Lord because of our children's deaths. There were some particularly heartrending episodes. Two weeks before their deaths, Kim and Melisa went to the altar and specifically prayed for the salvation of two people that they loved very much. "God, please save them, no matter what it takes." One of these people, according to her own account, has become an entirely new person. I know that Kim has said, "It was worth it all," because of this new found soul that she can spend eternity with.

About two weeks after the funeral I got a letter from a lifelong friend. Her parents and my parents were friends before we were born, so we were literally lifelong friends, yet we had not seen each other in years.

According to her letter, she had gone home from the funeral and just sat for days. As a mother of twin boys herself, she knew this had to be the most horrible experience of our lives, yet she could see our peace. She didn't understand it. I wrote back a very lengthy, inspired letter, explaining our salvation, our knowledge of the kids being with the Lord, and told how God gave the peace and that it didn't come from our own strength.

At the same time she had to call a girl that she barely knew about some matter. My friend, Lynn, told her of the funeral and her lack of understanding of the peace that we had. By coincidence, which I prefer to call one of God's many miracles, the girl was a Christian and they ended up talking for three hours. Lynn accepted the Lord and got saved. At first Dan, her husband, said, "This religion thing is okay for you if that's what you want, but don't try to shove it off on me."

Instead of pushing as she would have in the past, she sweetly said, "All right," and silently prayed. Within a short time, Dan began seeing the change and happiness within his wife, and began to desire what Lynn had. In just a matter of weeks, Dan too accepted the Lord as his personal Savior and, of course, their sons followed suit. Lynn is now a Bible school teacher and the whole family is growing rapidly in the Lord. I now had a deeper realization of the statement, "Don't you feel special?" God was enlarging His kingdom through Melisa, Kim and Dave. Praise the Lord.

At first we had numerous accounts of people being saved because of the kids' deaths. As time went on, Christians began telling us how they had drawn from our strength in their own times of need. Although we didn't think of ourselves as particularly strong and certainly didn't think of ourselves as having any greater faith, ability, or qualities than any other born-again Christian, we were grateful that God was using us. In fact we *knew* we were no stronger, holier, or more full of faith than any other born-again Christian. We were only five-year-old Christians when the kids were killed; we had done a lot of things right in those five years and a lot of things wrong. We were nothing special as Christians, yet we were something special. I think I realized that there is no average, run-of-the-mill Christian. Each of us is special in God's eyes once we become one of His kids. That strength others seemed to see in us was His strength, not our own. The great thing is that the same strength is available to all born-again Christians.

When I was a non-Christian, a baby of mine died. What I went through following his death was living hell. When these three died, what we went through was tremendous pain and agony, but not hell. God was always there with us.

Because we live in Nashville, Tennessee, the music industry is a part of our lives and a good part of David's law practice. Being Christians, much of our lives is wrapped around gospel music, a field of ministry from which so many of our friends make their livelihood.

Gospel music made an impact on our lives following the children's deaths. Andrae Crouch has a song that although we had heard many times, we didn't really hear until the kids were gone. It says, "Somebody told me that in sorrow they could be glad . . . but I didn't think it could be till it happened to me." The writer had an understanding of that fruit of the Spirit as told in Galatians 5:22. Only God can give that peace, which is a quietness and security in the face of adversity.

Only through Him is it easy not to become bitter and hard when life's blows become almost unbearable.

Our friends, Henry and Hazel Slaughter, sing at most all their concerts, "We've come this far by faith, leaning on the Lord; trusting in His holy Word, He's never failed us yet." How easy it would be to say, "Well, Lord, you really blew it this time; you have failed us." Yet, if we truly believe in God's love for us and His almighty wisdom, then we can rely on these words from a song, "We don't need to understand, we just need to hold His hand." I don't completely understand why God allowed our children to graduate to glory so early. Yet I know someday I will have a full comprehension of His perfect plan.

When we were brand-new Christians at Evangel Temple there was a young songwriter going to church there who had recently quit law school and come to Nashville to try his luck. Hundreds of aspiring writers, musicians and singers pour into Nashville every day, hoping to make it big, yet this young man had many of the necessary ingredients to become a success in the music business. One Sunday he sang a new song for the congregation that he had just written, "Lord, help me walk another mile, just one more mile. I'm tired of walking all alone. Lord, help me smile another smile, just one more smile. I just can't make it on my own." Little did I realize how a few years later that song would go over in my mind almost daily. Some days when getting out of bed to face the reality of daily life, when the daily lonesomeness seemed almost more than I could tolerate, my mind would say, "Lord, help me walk another mile, just one more mile. Help me smile another smile, just one more smile."

Two of our best friends, Barbara and Eddie Miller, have written many songs. Eddie's big hit was "Release Me." Eddie got saved about a year after we did, thanks to the prayers of his wife and daughter who had prayed for him for years. Eddie, like the man in the Bible, was extremely grateful for his salvation because his debt that was forgiven was indeed large. Eddie has tried to use his talents for the Lord ever since. One of Eddie's gospel songs contains this line, "What if He locks up the world and says that's all, this just might be God's last altar call." When we hear that, we are grateful that our kids made it to their altar call.

At Easter time of the year following our children's accident, Eddie Miller had his own resurrection day. At about 2:00 A.M. on Easter Monday, Mike Nelson, the associate pastor from the Lord's Chapel, called to tell us that Eddie had died. Mike knew we were close friends. David and I got up out of bed to be with Barbara. As we drove to the other side of town, in the stillness of the spring night, David and I began to think the same thoughts. Eddie was the first friend of our kids to go to heaven since they went there. In a strange way we were almost jealous of Eddie. We talked about Dave and Melisa competing to show Eddie their favorite spots in heaven.

We knew the first thing Eddie would want to do when he got to heaven was to meet Jesus, the one to whom he owed his salvation. In our minds we could almost see the kids so full of excitement and energy ready to share all of their past year's experiences in heaven with Eddie.

We were a little worried as we drove to Barbara's house, not knowing how she would take Eddie's death. In the five years since Eddie had been saved, they had been a very close couple who were devoted to each other. Like us, they spent almost all of their time together. They wrote songs and worked in other music-related activities.

When we arrived, we found that God had given Barbara that same strength that others had seen in us during the previous year. We all sat around the table that night talking, laughing and crying until it was morning and time to go to work. Joining us at Barbara's house were Barbara's daughter and son-in-law, and our associate pastor, Mike Nelson. If the unsaved world could have seen us that night they would have sworn we were "kooky." Although we mourn, none of us, including Barbara, had devastating, mind-breaking grief.

Instead, we spent the night talking about Eddie being in heaven. When Melisa and Dave were little, Eddie had a game he would play with them. He would often entertain them with this game in church, where he pretended he was pulling his thumb off. We wondered, out loud, if Eddie was pulling his thumb off in heaven for the kids. Mike said he bet on that Easter Sunday, God told the kids, "Get ready. Today is a big day because Eddie is coming home." We laughed about all the silly things Eddie had done and the things we had done together. Eddie had a great sense of humor and loved to tease. We cried because we would miss him. We prayed, not for Eddie, but for all of us, who would miss him.

Later Mike said it was the healthiest time surrounding death that he had ever experienced. At this time we more fully realized that quoting Scriptures is not necessarily what a Christian family needs when their born-again loved one dies. The family knows the Bible. What is needed is to create a mental picture of what they already know, that their loved one is in the presence of Jesus and is sharing eternity with those that went on home earlier.

Eddie's funeral was much like the praise gathering we had for the kids. Just as music was a big part of his life, it was a big part of his homecoming celebration also. The songs were written by Barbara and him, all giving praise to the Lord. The songs included "God's Last Altar Call," "Traveling Light on the Way to Heaven," and "Please Release Me from My Sin." Eddie always said that when he got saved so did his song "Release Me." Other songs included, "It's a Big, Wild, Wonderful Day, He Has Risen," and Eddie's last song that he had recorded, "Jesus, Let Me Write You a Song."

The entire few days of the funeral were great. People were saved, and still are being saved. I guess it was summed up by Eddie's brother-in-law who flew in from California. During the week, with so much prayer and praise surrounding him, he rededicated his life to the Lord. When it was time to leave, he told David, "This is a strange thing to say, considering the circumstances, but I have had a fantastic week." (I know Eddie loved that.)

Eddie knew the importance of gospel music. Like him, we have also gained much from Christian songs. The night of the wreck, a friend brought us the freshly cut acetate from a brand-new recording session. It was James Blackwood singing, "Learning to Lean on Jesus." This song has particularly been an inspiration to David. We do have to lean on Jesus, to be able to obtain from Him the power to go on with life. Possessing this strength keeps us from becoming emotionally handicapped. I suppose there are those who would say that our Christian belief is just a crutch. Frankly, we prefer that "crutch" to the ones used by the world.

Another friend of ours, Clay McClean, has written a song called "Plenty of Time." There is an interesting incident which inspired this song. One Sunday, Clay's teenage friend came to church and Clay talked to him about accepting the Lord as his personal Savior. "Naw," said the young man. "I am young and I have plenty of time to get saved, but right now there are too many things of the world that I want to do." This young man left the church service and was killed in a car wreck. The gist of Clay's song is that this young person doesn't want to accept the Lord because he is young and has plenty of time. But then his life is gone and he is now in hell with nothing but plenty of time.

Our children have plenty of time too—an eternity. When they have been there ten thousand years, it will have only just begun. But our children are joyfully sharing their eternity with Jesus.

Heaven is sounding sweeter every day, just like the song written by Levoy and Cleon Dewey tells us. "It's hard to lose a loved one to the grave but we have the blessed hope that Jesus gave. Heaven's sounding sweeter all the time."

Chapter 9

David and I had often felt that we had a definite ministry in the law office. We wanted to make Christ's presence apparent to those who came in. The law office is a great place to be a witness for many who come in are so ripe to hear the Word of God. When people are going through divorce, bankruptcy, arrests, and general problems, it is a perfect time to mention that Christ can see them through their trauma. Although it needs to be said in a more diplomatic manner than this, we must get the idea across that, "Look, you have made a mess of your life, you've tried everything else, now how about giving God a try at running your life?"

As lawyers we are able to see God at work within our law practice. There have been people who came in to see us, supposedly for legal work, that we just knew had been directed to us by the Lord. Once a man came in who had a financial problem. He was really down and out. In talking with him I was impressed that he had a desire to know the Lord, yet this desire was hidden beneath a rebellious attitude. Another of his problems was that he didn't know how he could pay me. Finally, I said, "I'll make a deal with you; I'll do this legal work for free if you go to a particular church next Sunday." This sounded like a good deal to him so he agreed. The next Sunday, he accepted the Lord as his Savior. This isn't my usual approach, but I felt led of the Lord in this case.

We had seen the Lord work particularly in potential divorce situations. There are times when divorce is the only solution to a difficult situation, if one or both parties have no desire to reconcile. Our aim, however, is to see marriages put back together, if at all possible. God has worked this out on several occasions. There is a certain pride in seeing couples, now happily married, who once were in our office for the purpose of obtaining a divorce.

We soon discovered that God had extended our ministry. We began receiving invitations to speak. To each of us He gave a different, yet coordinated, message. David and I had been so fortunate in that we enjoyed working together. In law school we took all of our classes together, and we started our new law practice as partners. Only after the kids were killed did I fully appreciate the parallel directions of our lives.

We had committed our lives to the Lord together, gone through the period of being young Christians, with more zeal than knowledge, grown into a maturity with the Lord at the same pace and, when this tragedy struck, we shared the same emotions. God gave us both the same peace, our healing process was at the same rate and our ability to share with others was now germinating simultaneously. My favorite phrase that comes from my husband is, "I married my best friend." Thank God for this love that is welded between us. We truly understand the biblical idea of being one flesh.

As I said, God gave us different yet correlating topics when we are invited to speak. If given a title, David's basic message is, "I know what kind of a day the Lord's coming back." David begins his story by telling the events which occurred on February 17, 1976.

David got up that morning and, as he did almost every morning, put on a pot of coffee. Then he turned on the TV to Barbara Walters on the "Today Show." Discovering that we had no milk, as often happens when there is a houseful of kids, he decided to go to the 7-Eleven store nearest us. He also wanted doughnuts to go with his coffee. It was pouring down rain and on the way he thought, "I must tell Kim to drive carefully this morning, it's slippery." When he got home, the kids were busy in the bathroom and his warning disappeared in his mind.

The kids told him good-bye; I had left, and he sort of poked around even though he knew I was anxious about his timely arrival at court for my trial. Since this was my trial, his head wasn't swimming with legalities as mine was.

Although he was running late, he decided to get gas at the neighborhood station. As he was paying for it and preparing to leave, an ambulance came by. It gave him a strange feeling and just then a second ambulance and a police car also roared past. This second ambulance gave him a sickening ache in the pit of his stomach. Without caring about his increasing lateness to court, David turned the car around and followed the ambulances. When the ambulances turned off the main road onto the country road which was the route the children took to school, the panic began to set in.

As he rounded the second curve, David was face to face with the sight of our demolished automobile and the truck, and he knew it had to be bad. He got out of his car and heard the sound of saws grinding away at the metal. He asked a police officer something unintelligible and stumbled back to his automobile. Instinctively, he drove to his parents and called me. The entire madness of what he had just seen hardly made sense in his state of confusion and shock.

David concludes his message by discussing the Second Coming. What kind of a day will it be when the Lord comes back? Why a day just like any other day. We will go about our routine doings, not expecting anything unusual; then suddenly the Lord will return and we will be united again with our children, as quickly and as surely as the instant impact that separated us from them. The very beautiful thing is that we will be united with them and Jesus will be the center of it all. The Bible tells us that we, as born-again believers, are joint heirs with Jesus. On that glorious day we will in fact receive our inheritance.

My message could well be titled, "If God's so good, why does He allow such things to happen?" In order to fully comprehend this question it is necessary to know more about the children.

Kim was a sixteen-year-old high school junior. She was a straight-A student. She was planning to enroll in college that fall because she had accumulated enough credits to graduate from high school. She planned to be a lawyer. She was a member of the student council, the choir, the senior play, the library club, and a class officer. She made the highest score in the history of the school on the college entrance exam. She was a very mature, refined young lady, and very much a fantastic Christian. She was involved in Bible study of all kinds, both by herself and in groups. She lived her life so that others could see Christ in her.

Dave, at thirteen, was a very bright and sensitive child who was an excellent student also. He had learned to do algebra before entering the first grade and began beating his dad and me in chess in the second grade. At thirteen everything was sports to him and he played basketball on the junior high team. He had been a good baseball player, having made the major league team of little league at age eleven. He loved the junior high scene and fancied himself to be the class comedian. He also planned to be a lawyer.

Melisa was twelve years old and she was another excellent student. In seventh grade she was president of her club, homeroom representative, first runner-up to the junior high queen, and she had represented her school in an area spelling bee and taken fourth place. She intended to be a doctor. Melisa was the one, when I came home from work, who would come flying down the stairs and throw her arms around me. I would say, "Melisa, I sure do love you." She would cock her head, toss her dark hair, her big black eyes would dance, and she would say, "I know it."

All the kids knew we loved them. This mutual love and

respect was one of the best things we had going for us. A security blanket of love warmed us all.

"Then, why," comes the question, "would God let this happen to three kids with such potential, who were loved and who had given their lives to Him?" The answer didn't start today, it started long ago. In the second chapter of Genesis, we read that God told Adam and Eve in the Garden of Eden that if they ate of the tree of knowledge of good and evil they would surely die. As the story goes, they did eat of the forbidden fruit, but they didn't die—at least not right then.

Since God is not a liar, doesn't it indicate that man was originally not meant to die? It was because of the sin of man that sickness and death have been passed down to the descendants of Adam. 1 Corinthians 15:21 tells us that by a man (Adam) came death, but by a man (Jesus Christ) came the resurrection of the dead. So, therefore, although the sins of man have brought the curse of death on us, through Jesus we can have life everlasting.

Now I don't mean to indicate that God was punishing us for our sins, by the deaths of our children. I mean that this whole death issue would not even be a reality but for the original sin of Adam and, as his descendants, death is passed down from generation to generation. By the same token, there would be no hate, war, violence, and other such problems, if there had not been the original sin of man.

The Bible says, "Believe on the Lord Jesus Christ, and thou shalt be saved" (Acts 16:31). Unfortunately, some have interpreted that verse to say, "Believe on the Lord Jesus Christ, and thou shalt be saved and live happily ever after." It doesn't say that. God doesn't promise us a rose garden after we get saved. If He did He would be no more than the Santa Claus in the sky. He does promise He will never leave us or forsake us. He promises to be with us in times of trial and He says the last enemy which will be overcome is death.

The Bible promises, "But when this perishable will have put on the imperishable, and this mortal will have put on immortality, then will come about the saying that is written, 'Death is swallowed up in victory' " (1 Cor. 15:54 NASB).

What does the word *believe* mean? Is it believing that Jesus existed? It must mean more than that because even the demons believe in Jesus and tremble. Then what does it mean? I think it means believing that He is God made into man, and believing that He is Lord of your life. I think it must mean that He is the almighty power that dwells within us.

We know that the kids' deaths were used mightily to bring about the salvation of others. Death was not a prison for our Lord, nor was it for our children. God seemed to say to both David and me some months after the funeral that He knew He could trust us with our burden. We learned, "In every thing give thanks: for this is the will of God in Christ Jesus concerning you" (1 Thess. 5:18).

This was brought home to me in the book, *The Hiding Place*. The Christian sisters, Betsie and Corrie, were placed in a German concentration camp under totally unimaginable conditions. One of the annoying conditions was the fleas that bit at them unmercifully. To Corrie's dismay, Betsie prayed and thanked God for the fleas. Although Corrie couldn't understand Betsie's prayer of thanksgiving, she respected her too much to question it. Later they discovered that they were able to have the forbidden Bible study and prayer in their compound because the guards wouldn't enter it due to the fleas.

We know that although we don't completely understand God's perfect plan, we are to give thanks and know that He is in charge.

The biggest step in my healing process came about in May and, after a time, I knew I had to share it with others. It was the day before Mother's Day, and it was a housework day, as

Saturday is for many working women. David and Jeff had gone off and I was alone with my thoughts of the Mother's Day without my children. I was low. I remember the many bouquets of dandelions I had received and the homemade cards with "I love you" carefully printed on them, and I cried. I would vacuum awhile and cry awhile, clean bathrooms awhile and cry awhile. I would sob and moan until my body would shake from the emotional strain. By night I fell in bed totally exhausted. About all I could pray was, "God help me," and He did.

My mind began to wander back to when my first child left for the first day of school. I had gone with her to enroll her and make sure she knew the way. The little neighbor boy, also a first grader, stopped and rang the bell. I watched Lauri leave the house and I went to the bay window in the living room to get a better view. I watched as her blonde hair flipped with each childish step and I watched her leave my world, entering her own, and I cried. But I knew I had to let her go.

Then I remembered one day when my son was about three years old and I heard him shout, "Mommy, mommy, come look at me." I ran to the back door and almost had heart failure as I saw that he was about five or six feet up a tree. My first impulse was to grab him down and tell him he could get hurt, but another part of me said, "No, he has to learn to grow up and if he falls he learns of danger and if he doesn't fall he learns of accomplishment." In other words, this is his world and he has to grow up in it, so let him go.

Then the Lord seemed to say to me, "It's the same now. They are with Me in this other world and you have to let them go." At that point I did something that produced much emotional healing, but it was the most difficult thing I have ever done. Although it was a mental process, it was just as real as if it were physical; I took each of their hands in mine, reached up, and put their hands in the hand of Jesus. Then with a great ache, I released my own grip, with my hand and let them go. I knew I had to give them to God and then let them go. I knew that once I gave them back, the bond between us was severed for the time being, and it was an act almost too great to bear. Yet it had to be done because they belonged to Him anyway.

When someone we love so much dies, it is extremely hard to let them go, yet I am convinced that at some point each of us must tuck the sweet memories of them into the corner of our minds and then let them go. But how much time must elapse before we are emotionally ready to let them go? I know it is not immediately after their death, yet for our own emotional healing to occur, it must come as soon as possible. I'm just glad God showed me relatively early that it had to be done.

Even now as I look back over every pang of hurt, every moment of grief and evey ache of lonesomeness, the most difficult task I have encountered, perhaps in my whole life, was the night I gave the kids to God and let them go. I still have difficulty containing my emotions, just remembering the scene. Yet, through this experience, I feel God has revealed to me an expansion of the knowledge that we must let them go.

In the law office we often encounter parents with teenage children on drugs and liquor. So often we see the parents who realize that if their kids would accept the Lord, this riotous living would be over. The problem is that the parents try to be their children's Holy Spirit. The parents try to convict their children of their sin, but that's the job of the Holy Spirit. The result is that their kids become resentful of the parents trying to force God on them. They resent being told that they are sinners, and the kids' reaction is to become more rebellious, to turn to more drugs and booze, and it becomes a vicious circle. From these experiences I have learned that many parents have problems with children, and as parents we have no other choice but to give them to God, and then let them go.

Lately God has let me see a further expansion of the concept of giving loved ones to God and then letting them go. So frequently we see problems where a spouse, usually the wife, has gotten saved and the other hasn't. Many times this creates problems within the marriage. Satan will try every trick he can to discourage a new Christian, and often he will use that person's mate. In many cases though the saved spouse creates his or her own problem, by trying to force this salvation on the other. That saved spouse needs to give the mate to God, and let go so God can work in the other's life.

This was seen in the case of Lynn, who got saved as a result of our children's deaths. She didn't try to force her newly found salvation on Dan; she just prayed and Dan saw that salvation in action and wanted it.

Then there was the case of Eddie and Barbara Miller. Barbara prayed for Eddie for years. She didn't have to tell him that he was a sinner. Eddie already knew that. God dealt with Eddie according to His own timetable. What became a beautiful husband-wife relationship, centered around the Lord, could have been the opposite, had not Barbara given Eddie over to the Lord.

There is another facet of this concept also. I had been thinking in terms of parents letting go of their children. I thought of the first time one of ours went away to camp and the anxiety I felt apart from them. I thought of them taking their first plunges into the deep water and I remembered sitting on the edge of the pool, waiting for their heads to pop to the surface, anxiously waiting to see if they were capable of swimming to the side of the pool. I thought of Lauri dating someone I didn't think was good for her, yet knowing she was old enough so that all I could do was tell her my feelings and then let her find out for herself. Even though she did indeed eventually find out, I worried each time she went out with him. But with all these experiences and many more, I knew that as a parent I would have to allow them the privilege of spreading their own wings and scraping their knees when they fell. It was in this way that they became fully alive and learned.

Our parents allowed us the freedom to grow and learn. Neither my folks nor David's parents are old, but what about all the people in the middle years who do have elderly parents? Are these middle-aged people preventing their elderly parents from having the freedom to live their lives and meet its challenges now that they are elderly? Each of us, to be motivated in life, needs challenges. To a child the challenge may be climbing a tree. To people in the middle years the challenge may be found through work or it may be found in painting a picture or redecorating a room. To the elderly the challenge may be getting through the day while keeping a sense of independence. When elderly people live alone there are risks; they might fall, they might forget to turn off the stove and they might forget to take a bath. But, without being able to meet these risks, there is also no triumph within them.

Many elderly people spend a lifetime bearing a houseful of children, raising and teaching those children, tilling the earth to produce the family's food supply, and canning every bit of food that was consumed by a houseful of hungry youngsters throughout the winter. They witnessed their children's marriages and may have seen some of their children buried. They lived a full life of love with a mate who might have been buried before them. After having experienced all of this in a lifetime, basket weaving for the elderly doesn't seem like a fitting finale. Shouldn't we extend the same privileges to our elderly that they have extended to us?

Chapter 10

The first anniversary of the children's deaths is now past. I am so glad that we will not have to experience any more first Easters, first birthdays or first Christmases without the children.

The opening of the box containing the Christmas ornaments and the kids' stockings wasn't as bad as I had thought it might be, although no stockings adorned our mantel this year.

We learned through our experiences that things we prepare for can be overcome more easily than the unexpected. It wasn't too difficult to get through the hard days such as Christmas, birthdays, and other special days, because we were ready for them. It was the unexpected things such as looking out the window one morning to discover the world in a winter wonderland of snow. Those first thoughts of how the children would gleefully squeal and run for the sleds would momentarily hit a hard blow.

Christmas this year did lack some of the excitement of previous years. Among our many family traditions has been our Christmas Eve praise program.

Each year, David's parents and my parents, his sister and her family, my sister and brother-in-law, and all the kids would gather together at our house. After stuffing ourselves at a big meal, we would assemble in the living room for our family program. First, one of the children would read the second chapter of Luke which tells about the birth of the baby Jesus in the manger. Then David's Aunt Mary, who is a retired Bible club missionary would tell a story with a flannel graph. Even as the children got older, we all looked forward to her illustrated story. Then the children would put on a program.

One year the children did a skit in which each played the part of someone approaching the gates of heaven to see if his name was written in the Book of Life. There was the one who was sure her name would be written down because she went to church every Sunday. Then there was another who was indignant that his name wasn't in the book because he had always paid tithes and contributed to charities. Finally the one who had her name written down was the one who had accepted Christ, but had no long list of good works. The kids had fun preparing this little story for our celebration.

The last Christmas with them, just weeks before their deaths, the theme of the Christmas program was, "Christ, the Glowing Hope." Aunt Mary's story centered around the glowing hope of the first coming of Christ. As the children were now a little older, they each in turn, stood up and gave a little talk on what Christ meant to them. Then each told when, and under what circumstances, they had accepted Jesus as their personal Savior. We were kept in the dark about their parts in the program and heard their testimonies for the first time on Christmas Eve. We sat there, our hearts bursting with pleasure and pride, as each told of his or her personal salvation.

After singing several Christmas carols, and listening to my sister sing some songs she had written, we would all gather in a circle and, in turn, each of us would give a prayer of thanksgiving to the Lord for His many blessings. When our program was over we would all be very full of love for God and grateful for His Son.

Shortly before the first Christmas after the children's deaths, Jeff said, "Mom, Kim, Melisa and Dave are going to have their first Christmas in heaven." He asked me, "What do you suppose it's like?"

I had to answer, "I don't know, son."

There was a faraway look on his face as he thoughtfully

continued, "I'll bet it's just great!"

As time goes on, we find that we like the term *Christian* less and less. People who were born into a Protestant or Catholic family call themselves Christians, and it has nothing to do with convictions. Just as there is an enormous spiritual gap between a Jewish person without convictions and a practicing, believing, Orthodox Jew who observes the law, keeps kosher, and reads his Talmud, there is the same diversity between born-again believers and persons who claim Christianity by birth.

I have often wondered if Jews, particularly Israeli Jews, know what a strong love born-again believers have for them. The born-again believer knows, because he knows God's Word, that the Jews are God's chosen people, and that Gentiles are "adopted Jews," through Jesus Christ.

I am convinced that America will survive in the last days only if it stands by God's chosen people. The Bible predicts that many countries of the world will turn against Israel. It is possible that turning against Israel will be the only way other nations will be able to buy oil from the Arab countries. This country has come out on top for two hundred years because it was founded on a basis of trust and faith in God, as set forth in those first legal documents of our country.

America is going through an unusual time in that we see the increase in violence and degradation within society, but, at the same time, we sense an increase in the forces of God throughout our society, especially within our government. This is no longer a token Christianity to make one socially acceptable, but a projection of a committed relationship to our Father within people considered to be the pillars of the community.

During this past year, believing lawyers are starting to become more visible. There is a new organization in Nashville of Christian lawyers. In the formative stages of this organization, while we were still trying to define our purposes, it was exciting to see that we weren't there for the purpose of becoming more socially acceptable to the general public. The goals that emerged from this planning session were: (a) to be a spiritual help to each other; (b) to learn more of God's Word as it relates to us and our law practice; and (c) to attempt to be a means by which our colleagues may come to know the Lord as their personal Savior.

I have thought that if the public could see this group of attorneys who range in denomination from Episcopal, Pentecostal, Baptist, Presbyterian and others, praising the Lord in unity, they wouldn't believe it. I'm sure those who want to find fault would call us hypocrites, but the reality is that these "stuffy old lawyers" are kids of the King, and are gladly admitting it. I'm proud to call them my brothers and sisters.

Through this past year we have come to realize the value of prayer. We have had literally hundreds of people praying for us and we know that those prayers have kept us strong throughout our time of trial. It has been possible to supernaturally sense the prayers of other people. It has been good to have Christian friends that call at nine o'clock in the evening, just when we were lonesome, to say, "Hey, come on over and sit by the fire." We're grateful for these people.

Life goes on. However, as long as we live, and have the capability to remember, the kids will live in our hearts. Life is a mystery, but we know who is the giver of life. Death is but a stepping stone to life everlasting.

Chapter 11

"I wish I had the kind of faith that you have," we often found ourselves being told. Often people seemed unable to understand how we could go on, working day by day without emotional calamities. Many times people would not seem to believe us when we told them that our faith was no stronger than what is available to any Christian. I've often said that if I had been asked the day before the wreck, "What would you do if three of your kids were killed," I probably would have said, "I couldn't take it." Probably the fact is that the day before I couldn't have taken it, but on the day I needed it, God's grace was there and it sustained me.

So often people have such a difficult time understanding salvation. People say, "Well, I'd like to get saved and have what you have, but I can't because—" and the reasons go on. I can't get saved because I smoke, I drink, I know I can't quit sinning, I'm having too much fun, I'm divorced." Then there are the other excuses—"I'll wait until I can live a better life," "I don't have the right clothes to wear to church," "I think you can find God on a hillside," "There are too many hypocrites," and many other similar ideas.

Salvation is so simple and that is the reason so many people believe they can't have it. We are conditioned to think that we can't get something for nothing and it is hard to conceive that salvation shouldn't be a reward. Yet none of us can get good enough to earn salvation. It's impossible. God didn't send His Son as a sacrifice for good people; He sent Jesus to save sinners. No one can work hard enough, do enough good deeds, or be good enough to receive salvation. It is purely and simply a gift, given to us by God's grace. God is there with an open hand, ready to give us this gift, but like any gift, it doesn't become ours until we assert our rights to that gift by reaching out and taking it.

Some have asked, "How do I take that gift?" It begins with a prayer to God, telling Him that you want to make Him Lord of your life, that you accept His Son as being a sacrifice for you, and accept Him as your personal Savior. Then ask Him to forgive you of your sins. The prayer doesn't have to take any special form or words.

Bells may not ring and cymbals probably won't clash when you say this prayer. If you accept salvation as a gift, believing in the Scriptures that if you ask you shall receive, then in time the assurance will come that you have become a child of the King.

Being too big a sinner is not the only hindrance to committing one's life to God. Occasionally we will encounter people in the office and elsewhere who are lulled into a false sense of security because they give to charities, help their neighbors, live a good life, attend church occasionally or regularly and, thereby, don't think they have to be saved. But it doesn't work that way.

In the third chapter of John, we read that Jesus was talking to Nicodemus. Nicodemus was a Pharisee, a religious leader of the Jews, but he was full of questions. Jesus said, "Unless you are born again, you can never get into the Kingdom of God." Nicodemus asked, "How can an old man go back into his mother's womb and be born again?" Jesus replied, "Unless one is born of water and the Spirit, he cannot enter the Kingdom of God" (John 3:3-5 TLB). We have to die to self and be born anew in the spirit.

The person who has two births, the birth of the flesh and the birth of the spirit, will only have one death—the death of self. Then at physical death we won't die at all, but will be spiritually changed and be in the presence of Jesus. However, if a person only has one birth, he will have two deaths, one physical and one spiritual. The Bible speaks of the second death of those cast into the lake of fire (Rev. 20:14-15), and the Bible says that those who overcome will not be hurt by a second death (Rev. 2:11).

When one does accept Jesus as Lord of his life, the first thing that happens is that Satan tries to get in and destroy this new relationship. Sometimes people will have a habit that they feel hinders them from God, yet they can't let go. Satan will get into the conscience and say, "See, you thought you got saved, yet look, you still have the same habits." The Bible doesn't say, "Believe on the Lord Jesus Christ and quit smoking and you will be saved." It tells you to simply believe and you will be saved. What the Bible does promise is that God will work out your salvation with you.

Then Satan puts us on a guilt trip. We sin and we ask God's forgiveness and know He said okay. Then we do it again and ask for forgiveness and know everything is okay. When we repeat the sin for the third and fourth time, and we ask for forgiveness, we begin to wonder if God is going to be in a forgiving mood. By the twelfth time Satan has us convinced that God's forgiveness is at an end and that we might as well hang it up and quit being a phony Christian. What Satan has done is to get us to look at God in human terms. We realize that if a friend or a spouse hurt us and then asked for forgiveness, we would forgive the person the first time, probably the second time, maybe the third time, but not the twelfth time. By then our patience would have given out and we would be most unhappy with the person that was hurting us. God can't be looked at from a human viewpoint. He is God, not a man. He has offered forgiveness and He is the same yesterday, today and tomorrow (Heb. 13:8).

Christ becomes our mediator and advocate with the Father. A lawyer is a mediator and an advocate for his client, in that he argues his client's case before the judge.

There is a judge in Nashville who has a father practicing law in the courts. Before we started practicing law we knew of a judge with a son practicing law in the court system. Needless to say, when a father draws his son's court or a son draws his father as judge, a different court must be requested. Why? Because there is a conflict of interest. The judge would tend to place more weight and more credibility on the argument given by his son.

We have the same situation when Christ is our advocate before the Father. God will sit up and pay attention to His Son when He argues our cases. That is exactly what Jesus does for us. When Satan takes us on a guilt trip for our sins and we seek forgiveness, Christ is there ready to say to the Father, "Yes, but he accepted Me as a full and final sacrifice for those sins. I have already paid the price for him."

People say to us, "I wish I had the kind of faith that you have." It is available, by making Christ the center of your life. People say, "I wish I had the kind of strength you have." That comes from God too, but it is acquired after much time and after many learning experiences. It begins with committing your life to God. Then you commit your marriage, your family, your business, your home, and everything else to Him. You begin each day by praising Him. Live one day at a time, acquire life experiences for that day, both good and bad, and use them as building blocks. Go to bed at night thanking Him.

One thing David and I have always had going for us, even B.C. (that is our way of saying before Christ came into our lives) is that we love each other. Like any marriage, we have had good times and bad times in our relationship, but the good parts were always in the longest column. We used the bad times to learn from, so that our marriage could become enjoyable. I have occasionally told David, "I've always loved you, but there have been times when I sure didn't like you." He has felt the same about me.

Once, early in our marriage, we had been fussing over some insignificant situation for two or three days. Finally

David said, "What would we do if we ever really had a problem?" This question was so emphatic that it has stayed with us. Here we were making such a big deal over such a minor issue, and it made us stop and think how we would handle a major problem.

When David and I were married, he said, "I can't promise you much, but I'll promise that you'll never be bored." He has kept that promise. One of the best things going for us is that we have a sense of humor. When we work, we work hard, but we have always put an equal vitality into play. I don't mean organized, game-of-chess-type of play, but teasing play—the running-barefoot-in-the-wet-grass-type of play. At our house, if one of us is watering the flowers, it is too irresistible not to spray the other. This is usually followed by a chase and a wrestling-type of hug.

David and I are also able to communicate. I love my husband for saying that he married his best friend. In our law practice we try to devote at least a couple of afternoons a month to each other. It may be for a romantic lunch or, perhaps in the spring, to go to the lake and fish (more appropriately, to drown worms). Our catch has included one rock, a rusty beer can, numerous weeds, two carp and one bass. The most important thing is that we talk—about anything and everything. We dream and we expound ideas and we feel safe in knowing that we won't be put down for dumb ideas.

Over the years we have developed a stability in our marriage. We both think, "You're important to me. I respect and love you and what you are."

When we made Christ the center of our marriage, all problems didn't automatically vanish but there were less of them. We learned to wait upon the Lord, and He has guided our paths.

When we were new Christians and so full of zeal, we wanted to do everything for God—all at once. We committed our lives to God in the spring. Summer brought vacation from law school, and we could go to church anytime we wanted without school interfering. Those midweek services were so great because they were teaching services and we had so much to learn about God and His Word. Each service opened up a whole new phase in our Christian experience. We were exploring God's Word with a fine-tooth comb and we were thoroughly excited about our findings. Jesus, the Israelites, the disciples, and the Pharisees all became relevant to us and meaningful for today.

Then came autumn and time to go back to school. When school began again, not only did our studies cut into our Bible reading, but classes cut into our midweek service. We began to feel as though the world of Christianity was marching forward, right past us, while we stood still.

We both became depressed and thought of quitting law school. We talked to our pastor who gave us some of the best advice we have ever received. It was advice that we have passed on to our clients on several occasions: "Don't ever make a decision when you are depressed or down."

When we were no longer down, we knew God didn't want us to quit law school. However, we still had the problem that we weren't getting as much spiritual food as we wanted, so we began digging it out for ourselves. Then we realized that you learn more if you dig it out for yourself than if you get it spoon-fed to you from a lecture. God's Word was implanted more deeply when we studied it for ourselves. Thus we reach another step in our spiritual growth.

As we grew, studied and settled down to a slow and steady pace of growth with the Lord, we began serving in various areas, such as teaching Sunday school. David taught young adults and I taught the senior high class. Our classes were challenging to us. We both found that there is no better way to learn a subject than to have to teach it. More than once they would come up with a question that would require us to say, "I don't know, but I'll try to give you an answer next week." We also taught Bible study in our home and in the homes of others.

We began visiting in other congregations and we learned many things. Some of these things were excellent and we incorporated them into our lives. Other things we learned did not seem to be of the Lord, and we knew that these teachings were not for us. One of the basic truths we learned is that the message of the gospel is simple and it doesn't have to be, and shouldn't be, made flashy and distorted. If that simple message of the gospel is told with love and praise, a church service can be a beautiful, warm experience.

We learned that God does miraculously heal because David experienced it. Back problems had bothered him for months after he lifted a boat onto a trailer hitch. Yet when he was prayed for he was completely healed. We also learned that all things must be taken in the light of reality. The fact is that not everyone who is prayed for gets healed, and there seems to be no correlation between the healing and the amount of faith displayed. I don't know why some get healed and others don't, but I know that a sick person who doesn't get healed doesn't need to feel condemnation for a lack of faith. As a matter of fact, this is one of the many questions I have to ask God about when I get to heaven.

We learned that as children of God we can be overcomers who are victorious over the world, but that doesn't preclude us from having a problem nor show lack of faith if we do.

We learned that we can trust God in all things. Sometimes there is a fine line between trusting God and tempting God. A story that illustrates this truth is about the couple that decided to trust God to multiply the gasoline in their car. They drove by many filling stations and couldn't understand it when they ran out of gas.

When Jesus fasted in the wilderness for forty days and forty nights, Satan appeared to Him and took Jesus to the pinnacle of the temple and said to Him, "Cast thyself down: for it is written, He shall give his angels charge concerning thee" (Matt. 4:6). But Jesus answered, "It is written again, Thou shalt not tempt the Lord thy God" (Matt. 4:7).

We also learned that God doesn't promise us a rose garden, just because we get saved. Heartaches come, but when you are committed to the Lord, good can and does come from all things, even our children's deaths. Souls get saved, lives become renewed and Christians are made stronger.

Chapter 12

One thing we learned early in our Christian experience was to establish priorities. Although I'm not saying that the priorities, as we have established them, must be followed by everyone, they certainly work well for us. In our lives, God is first, the family is second, our jobs are third, church activities are fourth and other things are less important.

We chose this particular set of priorities because we realize that if God comes first, then all other things fall in line. If He is the focal point of our lives, then outside problems of finance, health, fatigue, and other pressures are lessened.

Next to God, our family is most important. Our time here on earth is so short that we need to make the most of it by caring and sharing with our family. David and I want the times that we have with the remaining children, and with each other, to be always as pleasant as possible.

David and I are business partners, besides being marital partners. People often wonder how that could possibly work. Why shouldn't it work well? A partnership is a type of marriage anyway. Married people often know how each other think, so wouldn't that contribute to a successful business partnership? But whether in our business partnership or marriage partnership we have learned not to let petty things bother us. There isn't enough time here on earth to spend it arguing and complaining or letting resentment build. So David and I spend as much time together as possible and keep it as happy as possible. The moments we share together today are making tomorrow's memories and we want them to be pleasant.

Often we will see parents at a ball game or in the store

screaming at their kids. We ache inside and want to say, "Love them, don't build resentments, your time together is so short." When I was a young mother with small children I did that same screaming and yelling as harried mothers often do. I really thank God that I ended that long before our children went to be with Jesus.

Our jobs are a means of support, provide a certain sense of accomplishment, and enable us to be in a position to aid people. Yet our careers can't take priority over our family for, if they do, we destroy the very thing we are striving for. If our jobs take precedent over our family then we don't function well as a family. If there is unhappiness at home, we can't function well on the job. It becomes a circle of destruction.

We discovered that there can be a difference between working for God and working for the church. Working for God is an ongoing, twenty-four-hour job. Working for God involves our attitudes. We want to be available for God to use us at all times. Sometimes a determination to really work for God today versus being available when He wants to use us, can be the difference between disaster and success. When we decide to witness to ten people for God on a given day, we may leave some people with a feeling of condemnation because God's timetable wasn't right. However, if we allow God to lead us in a situation, He will provide the right words at the proper time.

Often people can get so involved in church committees, bazaars, programs, classes, and other activities, that there is little time left to talk to God and to read His Word. If David was given the choice of having me spend the day cleaning the house (working for my family), or spending the day with my husband and family, I know what choice he would make. David would want me to be with him. I think God would rather have us spend time *with* Him than *for* Him. Now, I'm not saying church work isn't important; it just shouldn't come before God or family.

In our law practice, we represent a lot of people with domestic problems. Priorities being out of place is one of the biggest causes of divorce. Women will say, "I don't understand why he runs around on me. I take good care of his children, clean his house, and he always has clean clothes. I never refuse him sexually, although I'll admit I'm not the sexy type." When the whole story is out what they really have said to us is that they have done all the wifely acts, except letting their husbands know that they are loved.

Similarly, the man will often say, "I can't understand why she should be discontented, I've given her everything. Why, I have worked twelve to fourteen hours a day just so she could have a fine home, nice clothes and so on." Again, what they have really said is, "I'm a success by the world's standard, I have a good position and money." What they don't see is that they have failed to provide their family with the things they wanted most—love and companionship.

Most of the harsh words that are spoken between spouses or parents and children are really saying, "Please love me and make me feel important to you." That is the real meaning of statements such as, "All you ever think about is your work"; "You spend all your time at the golf course instead of with me"; "You don't ever take me to dinner"; "Don't you ever care anything about the way you look?"; "All you want to do is drink."

Parents will often say to their children statements such as, "All you want to do is run around with your friends"; "Don't you ever want to spend time at home?"; "Why can't you ever clean up your room?"

Basically, all of us want to love and be loved. Yet, when we don't feel loved enough by our children, or spouse, or parents, we feel we can't just come out and say, "I want to be loved and you're not loving me enough," so we say everything else.

When we don't feel loved, it often becomes easy to think of ourselves as unlovable and we gradually develop a sense of not liking ourselves. When we don't like ourselves it is difficult to like others. Psychologists and psychiatrists say that the root of most antisocial behavior stems from the lack of self worth.

When the Bible says, "Love thy neighbour as thyself" (Matt. 22:39), the beginning of that has to be a feeling of self worth. Many Christians confuse boastful pride with self worth. Unfortunately, in many churches where negativism is preached, children begin to believe they are no good. It is true that we are all sinners, but by God's Spirit we are also worthwhile, worthy human beings. I like the Gaither's song that says, "I am a promise, I am a possibility, I'm a great big bundle of potentiality."

Children seem to live up to the expectations their parents have of them. If they are told that they are bad, they will tend to fit their behavior to that image. However, if a parent sees a small talent in a child and that child overhears mom tell her friends that he is good in art, the child will double his efforts to live up to her expectations.

When our children went to heaven, we had no time for regrets. For us to sit and say, "Oh, if I had only done this or that or if I had only said such and such," was useless. This would have only placed guilt burdens on us that we didn't need at a time of high emotional stress. Besides that, since they were no longer here on earth, we couldn't do anything else with or for them, so it was time to eliminate all thoughts of "If only—." Best of all, when our children went to heaven we could honestly say we had no regrets, because we truly loved them and they knew it.

I tend to be more conservative than David and when he suggests doing something, I often say, "Oh, David, we can't afford it." Now I'm grateful that he didn't always listen to me and that he insisted on some things. Some of the best memories we have of us all together before the children went to heaven were on the long weekends to Florida. We would pack sandwiches to eat in the car to avoid restaurants, and we didn't stay in the classiest places, but we made fantastic memories. I remember our tramps through the woods in the Smoky Mountains at Gatlinburg, and our trip to an Atlanta Braves game to see Hank Aaron hit a home run, and a day at Six Flags over Georgia. They are all such good memories that now I know that we really couldn't afford not to have gone. I'm glad David didn't allow me to let finances take priority over our beautiful outings together as a family.

Priorities became a big issue in a decision I had to make. Our law practice had increased to the point where we were financially in a much better position. Then suddenly I got a call from a local organization that was opening a new position which required a legal background. My name had been suggested to them. I was asked to come for an interview. I was told that they were also interviewing several men for the position. I went to a meeting with some of the top executives and they told me that this was a high-level, executive job and the salary and benefits were excellent. The people I would work with were fine men and it was a Christian-oriented organization. A few days later I got a call and was told that they had completed their interviews and I was the one whom they had chosen.

For days David and I thought, talked, prayed, and agonized over the situation. On one side, if I took the job, we had the potential for financial success in a relatively short time when we combined our earnings. I would be doing work that I thought I would enjoy; it would combine my legal knowledge with my past training. The organization was a fine one, with excellent colleagues. The position would also be a challenge.

On the other hand, David and I have worked side by side for many years. We took every class in law school together.

Upon graduation we turned down many job offers with firms to open up our own practice. We began our law firm partnership and built it together.

Working as we do we don't often see each other most of the day, but we still have lunch together and we are building as a unit. We also have the freedom, being self-employed, to arrange our schedule to spend some time together. We enjoy our jobs. When I get up in the morning I look forward to going to court or to the office. There are times when we get tired after a full day of hassles, but any job has that.

David and I finally decided that no amount of money was worth the satisfaction that we had from working together at something we enjoyed. Further, no amount of money was worth damaging our marriage relationship.

Besides all this, we have found that there is a definite need for a female Christian attorney. Many of my clients come to me because I am a woman who believes in Christ.

I guess the deciding factor came from Jeff. I thought we had carefully explained the choices open to us concerning this job offer. The next night, Jeff came home from school and seemed to place the whole situation in its simplest form when he said, "Well, mom, what is it, dad or money?"

I know to most people our decision would have seemed like utter foolishness. To us it was merely a decision to live according to our priorities. Again I was reminded of the "Lay up your treasures in heaven" verse (Matt. 6:20). If we managed to momentarily buy the world, what good would it do us if we lost the real parts of living—our relationship with God and each other.

Chapter 13

Although our story is told, it will never be told. The book of our life, as I perceived it, has been written. When will we get over our loss? We probably never will until we meet our children again. People come into our lives and when they leave we are changed. These three young people came into our lives, as part of us, and we are proud to have been a part of their lives. We did not know that we were capable of such deep love.

Do people have a premonition of their impending death? I think Melisa, the twelve-year-old, did. At Christmas, six weeks before her death, she made a plaque for her grandparents. On it she wrote, "I'm going to rise with the Son." She painted a pretty sun on it. After she died, I read Melisa's diary. She had visited some people she loved during her Christmas vacation. In her diary she wrote,

> Everyone is getting into the Christmas spirit, although it's more of the Santa spirit. It is supposed to be celebrating Jesus' birthday, but no one is. I know the coming of the Lord is near. When it comes people all over the world are going to be killed, and I'll be gone.
>
> I need God's help, I can't do it on my own. Every single person needs Him, but they seem to try to find it in other things like drugs. They search and pass by the real truth and only hope, God. I'll have to pray for as many as possible that their hope might be renewed.

I think I never really understood the depth of my twelve-year-old's relationship with the Lord until I read her words. Later she wrote as her vacation was coming to a close, "I hate to leave because I get this feeling that I'll never see them again."

Although I'm no prophetess or seer, simple logic and awareness of the times tell me that Christians are in for a hard row to hoe. If that be the case then my children are already home. Praise the Lord! Although the born-again Christian community is growing, denominational barriers are coming down and members from all denominations are becoming the Church. Satan, in all this, has a revival going on too. Satan's influence can be seen in records, movies, advertisements, magazines, and, most of all, in the media. Lately there has been an influx of movies and articles that make the Christian look foolish. The United States is being set up for religious persecution. If this course is continued we need to prepare ourselves with His words. Thank God we know the end of the book and we know who wins!

As Christians we must be prepared to face the problems of the world. The fact of the matter is that life's blows will sometimes knock us to our knees. From this vantage point we have two basic choices. We can either fall on our face in despair or use the time on our knees to gain God's strength and then get up and go on, stronger than before.

My reasons for writing this book are varied. I pray that God will be uplifted and given glory. I pray that through this book some will come to know the Lord as their own personal Savior. I pray that those going through similar circumstances will find the peace and healing power that we have. Perhaps, too, I want it to be a living memorial to our beloved children. For me it has been good therapy. Most of all, I have felt that the Lord wanted me to convey that the deep inner-healing process, even for born-again Christians, takes the dualistic form of victories and setbacks. The diversity of opposing thoughts and emotions are real and very much a part of us. Even the setbacks, when put into proper perspective can and do add up to spiritual growth.

A beautiful poem by Edgar A. Guest explains how I feel.

"I'll lend you for a little time a child of Mine," He
said,
"For you to love the while she lives and mourn for
when she's dead.
It may be six or seven years, or twenty-two or
three,
But will you, till I call her back, take care of her for
Me?
She'll bring her charms to gladden you, and shall
her stay be brief,
You'll have her lovely memories as solace for your
grief.

"I cannot promise she will stay, since all from earth
return,
But there are lessons taught down there I want this
child to learn.
I've looked the wide world over in my search for
teachers true
And from the throngs that crowd life's lanes I have
selected you.
Now will you give her all your love, nor think the
labor vain,
Nor hate Me when I come to call to take her back
again?"

I fancied that I heard them say: "Dear Lord, Thy
will be done!
For all the joy Thy child shall bring, the risk of grief
we'll run.
We'll shelter her with tenderness, we'll love her
while we may,
And for the happiness we've known forever
grateful stay;

103

But shall the angels call for her much sooner than
we've planned,
We'll brave the bitter grief that comes and try to
understand."

Awhile back, David had a court case with another attorney. The time for the trial arrived and the other attorney didn't appear, so the judge took other cases first. David checked to find out what was holding up his colleague and found that he was at the emergency room, because the end of his little girl's finger had been accidentally cut off. David waited throughout the morning for the other attorney's arrival and found himself getting impatient and irritable. All of a sudden, it hit him like a ton of bricks, "Here I am waiting on my friend, my colleague, another born-again brother, who would obviously be distressed by his child's accident, and I am more concerned about a lawsuit than how he feels." David said he suddenly became aware that that was also the way it was with our kids. At first people were greatly concerned, then later only our closest friends and family kept us in their prayers, and, someday, both we and the kids will be forgotten by most people.

So what then is important? "What then," you might ask, "is the reason for it all?" If it's all going to be forgotten, what I've done, what I've felt, what I've said, what is the reason for *me*? What was the reason for them, for our kids? What will be the ultimate product of what they did, what they felt, what they said, what they prayed?

Time spent on earth, if one lives a normal life span, is about a moment as compared to eternity. We can paint a picture, write a book, create a song to leave behind, but most people do not create such works. But even if a person does leave behind a book, picture or song, what will really count when the earth is gone? What legacy can we leave behind and also take with us? Life is only a training ground for eternity.

Those things we leave behind will all someday disappear, but those things we take into eternity with us will remain. There is an old saying that is very true, "Don't go to heaven alone, take somebody with you." We all influence others around us and we will neither go to heaven nor hell without taking others with us.

When we take others to heaven with us there is a snowball effect. The lives we touch and bring into eternity will touch other lives, and the pyramid effect goes on. Thousands can enter into the kingdom of God because of the testimony of one Christian. Jesus said, "What does it profit a man to gain the whole world, and forfeit his soul?" (Mark 8:36 NASB).

In my husband's attic, when he was a child, there was a plaque which belonged to his grandfather who was a preacher. I think it gives the answer to the purpose of life.

Only one life, twill soon be past;
Only what's done for Christ will last.